Preston So

IMMERSIVE CONTENT AND USABILITY

MORE FROM A BOOK APART

The Business of UX Writing
Yael Ben-David

Inclusive Design Communities
Sameera Kapila

Leading Content Design
Rachel McConnell

You Should Write a Book
Katel LeDû and Lisa Maria Marquis

Responsible JavaScript
Jeremy Wagner

SEO for Everyone
Rebekah Baggs and Chris Corak

Design for Safety
Eva PenzeyMoog

Voice Content and Usability
Preston So

Better Onboarding
Krystal Higgins

Sustainable Web Design
Tom Greenwood

Visit abookapart.com for our full list of titles.

Copyright © 2023 Preston So
All rights reserved

Publisher: Jeffrey Zeldman
Designer: Jason Santa Maria
Executive director: Katel LeDû
Editor in chief: Lisa Maria Marquis
Editors: Greg Nicholl, Danielle Small, Caren Litherland
Technical editor: Mat Marquis
Book producer: Ron Bilodeau

ISBN: 978-1-952616-28-0

A Book Apart
New York, New York
http://abookapart.com

10 9 8 7 6 5 4 3 2 1

TABLE OF CONTENTS

1 | *Introduction*

4 | CHAPTER 1
Content's Final Frontier

16 | CHAPTER 2
The Tech of Immersion

36 | CHAPTER 3
Content Immersion

67 | CHAPTER 4
Making Flow Happen

97 | CHAPTER 5
Ready for Liftoff

114 | CHAPTER 6
Beyond Content's Final Frontier

122 | *Acknowledgments*

125 | *Resources*

128 | *References*

131 | *Index*

For my mother,

이금란,

with love.

FOREWORD

DESIGN ENABLES US TO EXPLORE multiple viewpoints, share our views, and learn from one another. But immersive experiences—the kind that go beyond our screens and into augmented and virtual realities—are even more potent opportunities for fostering understanding, empathy, and dialogue. As we expand our content and design into the built environment, it's essential to consider the wide range of backgrounds, perspectives, and experiences that users bring to their interactions. It's imperative that we incorporate diverse imagery and inclusive language into our designs, and provide resources and tools that enable all participants to engage in accessible, meaningful conversations.

In this excellent guide to immersive content, Preston So shows us how to build inclusive, equitable, and accessible experiences across physical and virtual spaces. Ultimately, our goal should be to encourage participation and conversation. Immersive content has the potential to go beyond what we can achieve solely on a screen or through traditional forms of media, and to create a more engaging and interactive experience for everyone. By focusing on our users and their environments, we can cultivate more human and humane connections than ever before.

—Reginé Gilbert

INTRODUCTION

CONTENT EVERYWHERE. It's a grandiose idea, a lofty aspiration whispered for decades now. The information age demands we evolve our analog content—bulletin boards, public spaces, customer service kiosks—to become truly digital.

But is content *truly* everywhere yet, as many futurists breathlessly claim? Or is it still confined to the screen-based devices that decorate our homes and offices, merely offering momentary blue-lit glimpses into infinite information without truly delivering on that ambitious vision?

In fits and starts, content is voyaging beyond the rectangular portals in our pockets and on our desks by cementing itself within the world around us—whether that means the tangible universe we traverse day in, day out; or a virtual metaverse we escape to for comfort or recreation. Design is finally leaping past our pixelated screens with the elusive promise of *immersive content*, or content that plays in and with the space around us.

This book is about how to craft immersive content for a variety of contexts and situations. But it isn't an implementation manual or an all-encompassing almanac. Rather than focusing only on augmented reality or virtual reality or digital signage in isolation, we'll explore first and foremost how to design content with a sense of place—and without the arbitrary barriers of technology or jargon. As it turns out, you don't need to be an architect of buildings, a developer of games, or a scholar of mathematics to design effective, habitable immersive content capable of establishing authentic *presence*: that engrossing feeling of full absorption in a space.

Whether you're building a location-driven app that issues severe weather warnings or COVID-19 exposure alerts, or an in-store experience that lets customers summon product details as they browse racks and shelves, or a virtual environment that tells an interactive story in an alien landscape, immersive content doesn't just turn our square canvases into cubes; it also challenges us to look up from our devices and treat the universe around us as fertile ground for new insights in multimodal accessibility, usability testing, and inclusive design.

Case studies

Throughout this book, we'll examine and revisit a few case studies I led and designed several years ago while at the Boston-based software company Acquia with my innovation team, Acquia Labs. Since I'll refer to them repeatedly, here's a handy up-front guide to each project, identified in this book by the user personas they represent:

- **Airline passenger case study.** In this case study, we built a mobile app for hypothetical airline customers navigating an airport whose floor plan was equipped with signal transmitters at certain key locations. Our goal was to look at how the delivery of locational content triggered by these signaling devices could enhance an airport user's physical journey whether landing from, connecting to, or departing on a flight.
- **Grocery shopper case study.** With a mobile app we built and demonstrated for a national grocery store chain, a customer could scan items on shelves by positioning them within view of their smartphone camera. This action then pulled up a semitransparent overlay containing relevant content about that product.
- **College applicant case study.** In this case study, we created a virtual reality prototype that allowed prospective college students to tour a university campus entirely through an immersive headset without ever having to open a browser.
- **College student case study.** In this project, we designed content for digital signage dotting a public university campus that simultaneously accelerated wayfinding for new students and delivered pertinent copy drawn from the college website relevant to their current context.

Keep an eye out for references to these case studies in this book as we delve into how we designed and built them.

How this book is organized

This book lays a foundation for immersive content before touring through each phase of a typical immersive content project, in the following order:

- In Chapter 1, we'll define what immersive content is and what distinguishes embedded from environmental content.
- In Chapter 2, we'll understand how the technology underlying immersive content works and how to get started with it.
- In Chapter 3, we'll walk through why and how to design immersive content, whether that means writing new content or working with existing content, and what makes immersive content legible and discoverable.
- In Chapter 4, we'll look at three different ways to shape how users *flow* through immersive content: storyboards that establish narratives, flow diagrams that etch pathways, and spatial maps that fill in usable space.
- In Chapter 5, we'll evaluate our content for usability, accessibility, and safety, and discuss how to deploy and analyze our work after launch.
- In Chapter 6, we'll delve into what immersive content holds in store for us—both its risks and rewards—and how to ensure an equitable future for everyone.

As immersive content continues to permeate our physical surroundings—whether through vibrant digital signs and location-based pings, through semitransparent overlays that augment our reality, or through dreamlike visions that materialize a virtual world—this book will equip you with the tools and techniques you need to propel your content beyond the web and firmly into the world around us.

1
CONTENT'S FINAL FRONTIER

WRITTEN INFORMATION, throughout history, has always had to confine itself to the strict borders of some physical box, like every glyph in this sentence and every page in this book. Even in the digital realm, our experiences continue to be constrained by browser windows and shaped by smartphone screens.

Over the decades, we've become so accustomed to these boundaries that we scarcely notice them separating the content we consume from the world wrapped around us. Though these little boxes are entirely divorced from the environments in which we live, we've come to rely on them to define how, where, and why content begins and ends. For years now, we've had to interact with information on screens purely on their terms.

But what happens when we escape that bleak box? What happens when content is no longer something trapped in a glowing rectangle, but blends into the world around us as an integral component? What happens when the artificial shapes defined by our devices become seamless with the real-world spaces in which we've spent our lives?

IMMERSION

The answer is *immersion*: that elusive feeling of complete absorption in a place, whether that place is physical or virtual. It's the uncanny sense that what we do is in lockstep with where we are and where we're going—when we feel our experience of the world acts magically in unison with any user interfaces we need to work with along the way. Immersion is a flow state: our surroundings and our technologies are so in sync that we scarcely feel any distinction between them at all.

For virtual reality (VR) enthusiasts, immersion is about establishing *presence*, the notion that a virtual world is fully realized and imperceptibly different from the real world. But with all due respect, I'd argue that this focus on a single technology is far too narrow a way to think about immersion.

Immersion and *presence* aren't new terms, nor are they simply about bamboozling people into believing they're in a space they aren't. That's because immersion is much broader than VR and goofy headsets; it's about *encircling* and *enveloping* ourselves in an environment.

According to advisory and research company Forrester, *immersive experiences* are the subset of user experiences that erase "the boundaries between the human, digital, physical, and virtual realms" to enable smarter, richer user interactions (https://bkaprt.com/icu44/01-01). Immersive experiences, in short, unbind us from the proverbial box by unleashing content into the perceivable world. Their aim is to wipe away the experiential gap between our physical environs and our digital devices.

Immersive content is "content that plays in the sandbox of physical and virtual space—copy and media that are situationally or locationally aware rather than rooted in a static, unmoving computer screen," as I wrote in *A List Apart* (https://bkaprt.com/icu44/01-02). This definition accounts for all the directions immersive content both has gone and may go in the future, since the underlying technologies of immersion are constantly evolving and in a few short years may look nothing like they do today.

But what exactly do we mean by immersive content in the here and now? Here are a few examples of immersive content well within the realm of possibility today that you might have come across already:

- You've just disembarked from a flight for a tight layover at an unfamiliar airport. What if you could receive the right information about your connecting gate at the right time, and more importantly, in the right place, rather than fiddling around with the airline's website?
- You're visiting a grocery store and need more information about a product than is available on its label. You could go to the store's website to conduct a search or to drill down a list of categories, but what if you could simply scan an item on a device and see the relevant content materialize right alongside it?
- You're a high school senior applying to colleges, but you can't make any of the in-person tours that the admissions office provides. The university's website and print brochures give some sense of what campus life is like, but what if you could learn more by immersing yourself in a three-dimensional virtual campus experience?
- You've just enrolled in a large public university with a huge campus. While you could visit the website or mobile app to consult a map every time you need to figure out where you're going, what if you could access that information in real time as you navigate campus, whether via a device like a smartphone or via your environment?

In each of these instances, the unifying motif is information *stemming from the user's* location rather than information siloed away in a screen. Sure, we can access content at will on a smartphone, but that content can't help us where we are without first whisking us away into the foreign realm of a website or app.

At its core, immersive content has four key characteristics:

- **It's rooted in the physical world.** All immersive technologies have some relationship to the physical world off our devices, unlike interfaces that only inhabit smartphone screens and computer monitors. Whether text or media unfurls across a wall of television screens, unspools on a location-enabled tablet, or materializes through a VR headset, immersive content is inextricably linked with our actual, perceivable surroundings.

- **It typically involves signage or labeling.** The written content we encounter in the physical world largely falls into two categories: signage and labeling. *Signage* communicates a situational message. Think of departure boards in train stations or LED expressway signs that describe traffic conditions; even AMBER alerts and weather emergency notifications arguably fall into this category. *Labeling* conveys information about a product or service in our vicinity. It appears, for example, in nutrition facts and allergen warnings on food packaging or fold-out booklets on prescription pill bottles. Unlike analog signage and labeling, digital signage and labeling are dynamic and changeable, like arrival boards in airports, or product overlays hovering in a virtual department store.
- **It responds to movement.** When we move our bodies in a physical environment (when we, say, switch rooms in a museum or aisles in a grocery store), any websites we might be viewing at that moment don't usually change with us. But with immersive content, movement modulates what information shows up, how it's displayed, or where we see it (FIG 1.1).
- **It operates in three-dimensional space.** We consume most of our content today, from tabloid newspapers to retail websites, through two-dimensional means. But immersive content relies on three-dimensional canvases, whether they're our own bedrooms converted into beaches in VR headsets, or transit hubs that unveil shifting information on digital signs.

Some of our screen-bound content can also emulate these traits, and that's because our industry has long toyed with these core tenets of immersive content. Our devices can project three-dimensional spaces onto two-dimensional screens. Our smartphones react to how we move through our environment by tracking our location. What's different now is that our tech-

FIG 1.1: We interact with immersive content movements, positional or orientational changes in space, like this shift in a shopper's location in a grocery store.

nological landscape has matured to the point where we can finally jump off the screen and break out of the box.

EMBEDDED AND ENVIRONMENTAL CONTENT

The phrase *immersive content* is a bit of a misnomer because it straddles two extremes—embedded and environmental.

Much immersive content today remains confined to and embedded in handheld devices because, in most environments, it can be costly to erect screens everywhere or manifest holographics that are visible without the aid of wearable headsets, clunky accessories that overtake a user's entire field of vision but can be awkward and uncomfortable. Who wants to wear a headset day in and day out?

Let's walk through the two ways, embedded and environmental, in which people will come across immersive content:

- **Embedded content** is text and media accessed strictly within the frame of devices. This might mean a push notification conveyed to our smartphone based on our location, or an overlay projected onto the camera view of our iPad as we brandish it before us. Embedded content is narrowly outlined by the *in-device* perspective of our smartphone and

tablet screens, which amount to a scanty subset of our full field of vision.
- **Environmental content** is text and media that we perceive as an ambient element of the world around us, part and parcel of how we experience our spatial surroundings. This includes digital signage that we squint at from a distance on a subway platform and content displayed inside a VR headset. Environmental content encircles us by emerging or materializing in the *in-world* perspective of our own eyes and ears—one and the same with how we normally live our lives.

In other words, environmental content requires explicitly three-dimensional approaches to design content, whereas embedded content is devised for three-dimensional situations mediated through two-dimensional interfaces. But there's some important nuance here.

Our smartphones can straddle the line between embedded and environmental content by turning on a dime between two states of being, so to speak. After all, smartphones are devices we keep in our pockets, serving us embedded content when we need it as a momentary portal into information, a finite corner of our worldview. But the same smartphone can also morph into a fully immersive VR headset. Take Google Cardboard, a do-it-yourself VR headset consisting of a phone and a few pieces of cardboard, enabling users to swap between embedded and environmental forms of interacting with content by snapping the device in or out of the cardboard casing at any moment.

Likewise, content itself can respect or blur the distinction between embedded and environmental contexts, especially when it comes to interface text. Some video games, like the postapocalyptic series *BioShock*, display both embedded text to indicate certain conditions of the player character (the amount of currency or the items they have available, for example) and environmental text to reveal critical insight about the world (such as books that need to be read to unlock clues or signage that points to a place of interest nearby).

Even VR experiences draw a clear line between embedded help text, which gives the user guidance about how to control overlays and other interface elements, and environmental ambient text, which informs the user about the world they're exploring, such as through maps or signage within that world. In other words, embedded content in VR is like the speedometer or fuel gauge in a car, while environmental content is the signage and billboards that whoosh by in the windshield.

This key distinction between embedded and environmental content is critical to how users perceive and interact with the information present in a space. But just as fundamental to where designers choose to nestle content—whether within the confines of a handheld device screen or as a figment of the perceivable world—is how users navigate it. And because immersive content is spatial at its core, navigation necessarily involves motion: changes in position and orientation.

LOCOMOTION

When we roam the immense user interface that is our world, we engage in *locomotion*, or movement from one place to another. With immersive content, locomotion is how we connect discrete pieces of content relevant to one spot but not another. For instance, driving across a national border might prompt a smartphone notification saying we've switched from miles to kilometers, just as an analog sign by the highway would. Pointing a phone camera at two separate products in a supermarket aisle might highlight differences between them, in the same way that picking each up in our hands would allow us to compare their worth.

For the most part, real-life locomotion modulates how we view and understand the world and thus undergirds all immersive content, whether that means digital signage, augmented reality, or location-driven content. That keeps things simple for us. But virtual reality frequently demands a different form of navigation. After all, ignoring the very solid barriers and hazards strewn throughout the real world is a recipe for accidents and injuries.

Moreover, virtual worlds can feasibly be much more extensive than even the entirety of our own planet's surface area, since their farthest extremes are potentially the limits of our imagination. In Chapter 2, we'll talk more about how VR realizes locomotion, but suffice it to say for now that locomotion can involve real human movement like the use of our legs or a wheelchair, or, out of necessity, *imagined* movement that isn't reasonable for any person in real life. After all, immersion isn't just about space; it's about the relationship real people have with that space. That's why from the get-go we also have to talk about how to make immersive content as human-friendly as possible.

THE HUMAN SIDE OF IMMERSIVE CONTENT

Immersive content is so compelling because it connects us humans more deeply with our surroundings. Existing work in architecture and urban planning can teach us a great deal about how our users interact with spaces both familiar and unfamiliar. And we can also stand on the shoulders of those who have studied immersive experiences' impact on health, accessibility, and society. Let's examine *why* we construct physical spaces in the first place: for the benefit of humans and other animals.

Spaces can be hostile or hospitable

Collectively, all the masonry and earthworks we've amassed over millennia are known in architectural and urban planning circles as the *built environment*: every space converted from its natural state to a new artificial form to facilitate human activity. Most people in the modern era live the entirety of their lives fully within this built environment.

The built environment shapes how we move through a space. Speed bumps slow drivers down, raised crosswalks protect pedestrians, and rumble strips on highway shoulders keep motorists from veering off course. These techniques are a testament to how physical spaces can take on a personality of their own. And broadly speaking, these methods aren't tied solely to our analog environments; we deploy them in digital contexts too.

But not all aspects of the built environment are positive. *Hostile architecture*, for example, uses the built environment to discourage interaction from people whom those with authority and power find undesirable. These tactics might include spiked surfaces to prevent unsheltered people from sleeping, slanted benches to deter skateboarding, and barbed-wire fences to obstruct access to public spaces.

Beyond determining how useful physical spaces are, hostile architecture can also extend to how we present content in them as well. Commuters don't just knock New York City's Penn Station for its labyrinthine layout and low, claustrophobic ceilings; its inconsistent mix of analog and digital signage (the result of territorial splits between transit agencies with unique design systems) is also a target of derision. More recently, Penn Station's renovation and Moynihan Train Hall expansion attracted withering criticism for a lack of seating. Designed to keep unsheltered people out, the "exclusionary design plan [also] punishes transit users," particularly the elderly and disabled, as well as those with injuries and small children (https://bkaprt.com/icu44/01-03).

As designers, we can only do so much to influence how public spaces are planned, but how they convey information, especially on devices, is our domain. And today, the built environment we control is digital, virtual, and immersive. Immersive content design is an opportunity to enrich our spaces—or thwart the very people we're trying to help.

Safety and immersive content

When we design content for immersive environments, we have to pay particularly close attention to the physical health and safety of our users. Unlike interacting with web and mobile content, where screen fatigue and carpal tunnel syndrome rank among the only serious potential health consequences of consuming information, interacting with immersive content can result in significant bodily injury.

Any embedded content housed in devices requires users to switch contexts quickly between the inner cloister of a smartphone or tablet and the outer milieu of physical environments.

This can lead to falls and crashes with other people. For example, researchers in Japan discovered that users who walk while using their cell phones disrupt the flow of people around them (https://bkaprt.com/icu44-01-04, behind paywall).

Environmental content, too, can pose dangers. Digital signs positioned in areas where there isn't sufficient clearance to stop for a moment to read can lead to crowd collisions and bottlenecks at key points. As we'll see in Chapter 4, this is an important reason to diagram your users' flows and map your spaces to avoid hurdles in high-traffic areas.

VR headset users aren't immune to physical hazards either. Those who move around a virtual space without guardrails can bump into obstacles in their vicinity; sudden appearances of VR overlays or other elements can jolt them so much that they stumble or fall. Moreover, VR interfaces can cause *virtual reality motion sickness*, also known as *visually induced motion sickness* (VIMS), in which people experience symptoms such as dizziness, nausea, and other issues like disorientation, headaches, and blurred vision, as Steve Aukstakalnis wrote in *Practical Augmented Reality* (https://bkaprt.com/icu44-01-05). VR experiences can also cause vertigo, depending on the content; flickering imagery that occurs faster than one flash per second, whether it occurs in real life or within a VR headset, can cause epileptic seizures (https://bkaprt.com/icu44-01-06).

These physical health impacts aren't the only ways that immersive content can cause harm for users. Just as many of our physical spaces are designed for a nonexistent "average" user—one who is non-disabled, young, cisgender, straight, white, and male—much immersive content falls into the same trap. As such, we end this chapter with an exploration of how to consider issues of equity and inclusion in your immersive content from the very beginning.

Inclusive and accessible immersive content

In a society where systemic oppression is as much a fixture as the built environment, designing immersive content inclusively, equitably, and accessibly is paramount. Inadvertently or not, our content can be anti-Black, racist, misogynistic, queer- and transphobic, ableist, ageist, and otherwise discriminatory along dimensions we might not immediately recognize, thanks to long-established biases in our industry.

Machine vision that identifies people based on physical attributes can demonstrate prejudice against historically excluded groups, especially Black and Brown people. That bias can show up in a variety of settings, like the infamous touchless soap dispenser in a Marriott hotel restroom that couldn't detect Black skin (https://bkaprt.com/icu44/01-07); or in more nefarious situations, like flawed facial-recognition software leading to wrongful arrests of innocent citizens (https://bkaprt.com/icu44/01-08, behind paywall). Disabled people, too, face specific barriers to locomotion and interacting with manual controls that warrant attention at all stages of a project.

Inclusive and equitable immersive content must start with centering and giving space to people with historically excluded communities. They need not only a seat at the table, but also meaningful control over their interactive experiences.

Immersive content can be rendered entirely inaccessible if wheelchair users can't reach it, or if colorblind people can't distinguish text from its background. For Blind and low-vision users, aural equivalents for content are a baseline requirement. For elderly people or users of mobility aids, both the content we deliver and the spaces we design must account for differences in locomotion. Though we'll discuss accessibility testing at length in Chapter 5, suffice it to say that accessibility should be a primary consideration from the moment your project kicks off all the way through its final stages.

Some immersive experiences not only hamper the ability of historically excluded people to retrieve key content; they also directly harm them by treating them in ways that reinforce structural oppression, such as algorithmic racism in machine vision. If you must use machine recognition of an individual to deliver immersive content—something I'd strongly urge teams to find alternatives for—ensure that the underlying algorithms aren't rooted in mechanisms that perpetuate anti-Blackness and other forms of racism. Err on the side of leveraging machine vision solely for inanimate objects, because, like other unintentionally problematic technologies, it can dehumanize the users you're trying to serve.

We also have an opportunity to improve representation of historically excluded communities in immersive content, especially given that technologists have often adopted crude methods to forge human identity in immersive environments. For instance, some firms entering the nascent metaverse market are creating "virtual human" characters driven by artificial intelligence (AI). They are by and large presented as cisgender heterosexual women catering to the male gaze—like Ana, a hyperrealistic AI woman created by video-game publisher Krafton for their metaverse (https://bkaprt.com/icu44/01-09). These characters, however helpful they may be to users, bolster problematic notions about women and other oppressed groups in our society, much like the virtual assistants Alexa and Siri did before them.

We can't embrace all identities unless we welcome them to the table to begin with, as we'll see again in Chapter 6. Without true representation everywhere, we can't have true content everywhere.

TRUE CONTENT EVERYWHERE

The web has long served as a source of boundless information broadcast into virtual spaces—but browsing the web feels more like leafing through a magazine or newspaper than stepping into another world. For a long time, content that could break out of our screens and integrate into our environments has been considered a futuristic figment of the imagination.

But immersive content is no longer a gimmick. We can now deliver information optimized for human interaction everywhere, in both physical and virtual spaces. Now that we have a rudimentary understanding of immersive content, let's dive into the current state of the tech that makes it all possible.

2 THE TECH OF IMMERSION

GROWING UP AS A MILLENNIAL, I was surrounded by futuristic visions of immersive content in science fiction and fantasy. I recoiled at the nightmarish iris trackers of *Minority Report*, which allowed highly targeted advertisements to assail passersby by name. I marveled at the unbridled possibility of *Star Trek*'s utopian holodeck, a fictional device capable of simulating real and imaginary worlds by manipulating light and energy. The holodeck exemplified a fully immersive virtual reality, not only for the modalities of sight and sound, but for all senses, and without the inconvenience of wearable gear.

Some of these ideas, for better or worse, have come to life sooner than others. *Minority Report*'s personalized popups and intrusive banner ads emerged quickly on the web, and at Detroit Metro Airport, Delta Air Lines has deployed what it calls a PARALLEL REALITY™ experience, which displays content about a passenger's upcoming flight on their smartphone when standing below overhead digital signs (https://bkaprt.com/icu44/02-01). But dreamier visions like *Star Trek*'s immersive holodecks are still years away.

FIG 2.1: Digital signage content (content in space).

Because the technologies underpinning immersive content continue to evolve, our ideas of immersive content have to straddle both what's within reach today and what yet lies in the far-flung future. But established categories of immersive content technologies already exist in the here and now:

- Digital signage content (**FIG 2.1**)
- Locational content (**FIG 2.2**)
- Extended reality content, including augmented reality (**FIG 2.3**) and virtual reality content (**FIG 2.4**)

Before we classify immersive content into distinct types, remember that these labels can do us a disservice as designers, because we can, in many cases, blend multiple forms into a single cohesive immersive experience. Since immersive content is about erasing the arbitrary lines drawn between screens and the three-dimensional world, resist the instinct to divide immersive content into device-bound categories.

FIG 2.2: Locational content (content at a movable point in space).

FIG 2.3: Augmented reality content (content projected into real-world space).

FIG 2.4: Virtual reality content (content projected into virtual space).

DIGITAL SIGNAGE: CONTENT IN SPACE

Unlike *analog signage* (static signage not mediated through a screen), which has long been a cornerstone of the built environment, *digital signage* uses screens and moving images to transmit information relevant to people in a given place—and it's one example of immersive content that many users have already encountered in the wild. Digital signage content is true *content in space*.

Digital signage feels like an overly simplistic example of immersive content because it's a recognizable bridge between screen-bound and immersive experiences. There's a broad spectrum of digital signage too, since airport baggage carousel jumbotrons can share space with touchscreen kiosks specific to individual travelers' needs. Regardless of the content they deliver, digital signs are coupled tightly with how we interact with physical spaces, whether we consult them with a quick peripheral glance while in motion or a slow tap-by-tap lookup while lost and standing still. In *Unleashing the Power of Digital Signage*, Keith Kelsen distinguished between three types of

THE TECH OF IMMERSION   19

digital signage of interest to content designers (https://bkaprt.com/icu44/02-02):

- **Point-of-sale digital signage.** Often found adjacent to supermarket aisles and department store racks, point-of-sale digital signage entices a shopper to consider a product or a range of products.
- **Point-of-transit digital signage.** Point-of-transit digital signage is typically encountered where people are in transit, such as on trains or buses, or as they pass by storefronts. Kelsen refers to these broadly as "digital billboards."
- **Point-of-wait digital signage.** Point-of-wait digital signage is found when people are queueing for a product or service, such as waiting in line at a bank, hospital, or hotel.

But digital signage content doesn't need to be bound strictly to screens. Today, digital signs are jumping off the screen in unexpected ways, like *projection art* that subversively conveys protest messages by commandeering or challenging official messages from governments and institutions (https://bkaprt.com/icu44/02-03). In the future, they could become holographic or even three-dimensional, transcending what they're capable of today. Therefore, we should be wary of the arbitrary distinction between what screens can do at present and what digital signage may look like in the future. That's partially why Kelsen refers to digital signage as the "fifth screen" after motion pictures, televisions, computers, and cell phones—it doesn't fit neatly into any of those screen-bound groups.

LOCATIONAL CONTENT: CONTENT AT A MOVABLE POINT IN SPACE

Whereas digital signage is most often deployed for many users at once in physical spaces, sometimes more personalized, location-specific content is appropriate. All personal devices today—smartphones, tablets, and computers—can receive content based on *geolocation*, the triangulation of a device's geographical

FIG 2.5: In this example of locational content, beacons strategically positioned throughout a menswear store trigger the delivery of push notifications to a shopper's device depending on where they are on the sales floor.

---

location based on cues such as their proximity to transmitters or pings from satellites. *Locational content* is immersive content (like push notifications, in-app notifications, or text messages) whose delivery depends on a user's whereabouts—*content at a movable point in space.*

Many brands today already use locational content to deliver information directly to our smartphones in shopping malls and brick-and-mortar department stores (**FIG 2.5**). Personalized content finds us by tracking not only our online preferences, but also our real-time locations. Of course, this raises huge concerns for our privacy as users. Locational content can be used to instruct a user to test and self-isolate when they've been in close contact with someone who has COVID-19, or alert them to the nearest place where they can seek medical attention.

Currently, most locational content relies on one or more of the following mechanisms available on personal devices, in ascending order of accuracy:

THE TECH OF IMMERSION 21

- **Network-based phone tracking.** Before the advent of GPS capabilities on mobile phones, the most accurate way to deduce a person's location was through cellular networks. Base stations and cellular network nodes, which are more densely packed together in urban areas, are hubs of communication for all wireless devices in the region, and can be used to deliver information like emergency alerts to all phones and tablets in a particular range.
- **Bluetooth low-energy beacons.** Bluetooth low-energy (BLE) *beacons* are small battery- or USB-powered devices—often no larger than a computer mouse—that transmit information about themselves to wireless devices in the immediate vicinity. BLE beacons are notoriously finicky and imprecise, and need to have Bluetooth enabled at all times to function. Until the privacy concerns inherent to leaving Bluetooth on (which can sometimes leave device backdoors ajar for attackers) find better solutions, beacon use remains fairly niche, though many are taking advantage of the paradigm nonetheless.
- **GPS location tracking.** All modern wireless devices can send and receive information using the Global Positioning System (GPS), a satellite-based network for geolocation used around the world. When you turn on location services on your phone, for instance, GPS is one of the key ways devices understand your position in the world.
- **Wi-Fi positioning.** Today, especially to track a user's location indoors, most mobile devices use a mix of GPS location tracking and Wi-Fi positioning to glean the most accurate possible location of your phone or tablet. Wi-Fi positioning systems (WPSs) rely on Wi-Fi hotspots and wireless access points nearby to know where you are, especially in interior spaces where GPS signals tend to be blocked.

One advantage locational content has over other types of immersive content is that it's largely grounded in mechanisms of content delivery that designers are already familiar with: push notifications, SMS messages, and other short dispatches of information. The bigger challenge lies in cleanly associating that content with the user's whereabouts. That's why many organizations opt to couch locational content within a surrounding user experience, such as a mobile app, that can present that additional context.

EXTENDED REALITY: CONTENT PROJECTED INTO SPACE

For many of us, the first thing that comes to mind when we think of immersive technology is *extended reality* (XR), a continuum of experiences layered onto or fully supplanting our real-world surroundings. A subset of XR is *mixed reality* (MR), which interpolates elements that don't exist into our real world, or elements that do exist into a virtual one.

Both terms represent a spectrum, known in human-computer interaction circles as the *reality-virtuality continuum* (**FIG 2.6**), which includes several subsets between the two extremes of "full reality" and "full virtuality":

- *Augmented reality* (AR) involves the insertion of virtual elements into a real-world environment—*virtual stuff in the real world*, whether that means a device that only partially overtakes our field of vision (like a smartphone camera view of the physical world with some virtual stuff on top), or one that replaces it entirely (like a VR headset displaying the physical world through video with some virtual stuff on top). In short, AR consists of virtual elements that augment the physical world, whether perceived through our own eyes or mediated through a device.
- *Augmented virtuality* (AV) is the opposite of AR: the insertion of real elements into a virtual space—*real stuff in a virtual world*. In AV, elements of the real world are superimposed on a virtual environment that we currently have no choice but to experience through a VR headset. In short, AV consists of real elements that augment a virtual world, *necessarily* mediated through a device (though this may change in the distant future).

```
                        Mixed reality
                            (MR)
              ┌─────────────┴─────────────┐
   ◄──────────┼───────────────────────────┼──────────►
   Reality    Augmented         Augmented          Virtual
              reality (AR)      virtuality (AV)    reality (VR)
              virtual stuff in  real stuff in
              the real world    a virtual world
              └───────────────────┬───────────────────┘
                            Extended reality
                                (XR)
```

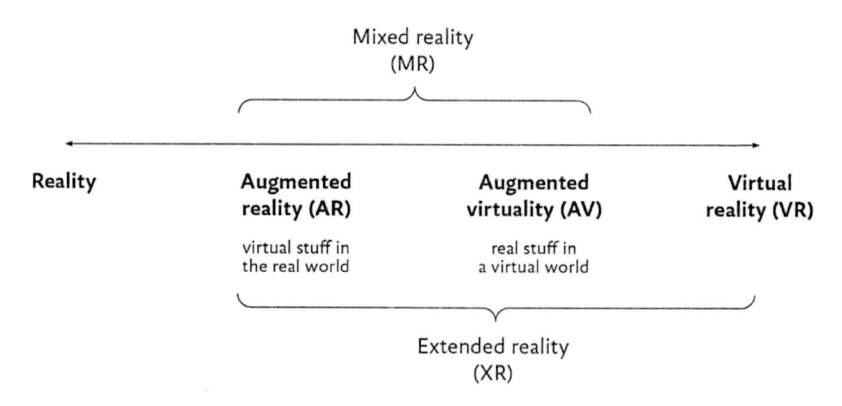

FIG 2.6: The reality-virtuality continuum, which depicts the continuum of possible extensions to the real environment in the form of extended reality and the melding of a fully real and a fully virtual environment in the form of mixed reality.

- *Virtual reality* (VR) involves the creation of a fully immersive virtual environment that we perceive to be just as real as the physical world, and where none of its elements exist in reality. VR consists of *virtual stuff in a virtual world*, also for now necessarily mediated through a VR headset.

At present, immersive designers working with mixed reality are generally more concerned with how to introduce virtual-world elements into the real world (an AR experience), rather than how real-world objects can figure in a virtual world (an AV experience). That's because there's less demand for AV use cases, and the technology for it isn't quite there yet.

AR content: content projected into real-world space

Augmented reality (AR) content is stuff that's projected into real-world space, whether that means objects that don't actually exist or semitransparent *overlays* displaying information that are superimposed on top of what's in our surroundings. These overlays can be static and unmoving no matter how we orient or position ourselves, or they can be dynamic, adjusting

FIG 2.7: This display in the Museo Soumaya in Mexico City acts as an entry point for museumgoers with instructions to download an app to access AR content, and says in Spanish: "Discover exclusive content in augmented reality from your smartphone or tablet!"

---

to our orientation and position as if they existed in our real-world environment.

AR content allows us to associate content directly with tangible, real-world things, enriching our interactions with those elements. For instance, AR overlays are now commonly used in conjunction with museum exhibits, such as in the Museo Soumaya in Mexico City (**FIG 2.7**). Smartphone and tablet cameras allow us to access content through *machine vision*, or the ability

In-device augmented reality
(embedded)

In-world augmented reality
(environmental)

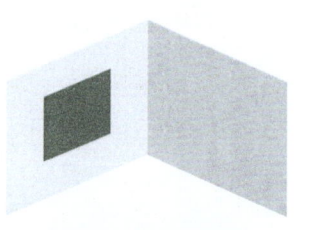

FIG 2.8: AR content can either be embedded in devices, where overlays and other elements are projected over the device's view of the real world, or it can be environmental, in which overlays and other elements adapt to and become enmeshed with the real world.

---

to identify an object in a photo or video. Holding our cameras aloft, we can now instantly receive embedded information about any item we've trained our focus on, like a medieval painting.

AR content is both complex and exciting, not just because of the difficulties surrounding its design, but also due to its current technical limitations. Since we can't yet materialize opaque holograms of text, images, and video into thin air, we must make do with the devices we have. This means leveraging camera-equipped smartphones and tablets capable of displaying either embedded content that stays fixed to the device screen, or environmental content that adapts itself to the world around it (**FIG 2.8**).

Another option is to use headsets merging together real and artificial elements into a single world we perceive as video before our eyes. These two alternatives to the holographic ideal have a video camera in common, but at the moment, most AR content is smartphone- or tablet-bound rather than displayed through headsets, owing to the practical challenges of keeping them on for long periods of time.

But what happens when our device cameras completely overtake our view, becoming one with the visible universe and showing us nothing but stuff that doesn't exist in real life? That's where virtual reality comes in.

VR content: content projected into virtual space

In many ways, virtual reality is the culmination of immersive experiences. VR content is the text and media that decorate fully virtual spaces. It may contain the same semitransparent overlays we see in AR content—but whereas AR content is tethered to existing physical objects, VR content has no such worldly limitations. It may hover in virtual environments, be splayed across walls, or be molded into complex shapes.

Though future VR technology may advance to the point where holograms become a perceivable part of our unadorned reality, today, VR content still obligates the use of headsets (**FIG 2.9**). In the next few years, newer wearables that outperform VR headsets and prioritize comfort and long-term wear will likely appear, such as contact lenses that double as VR interfaces (https://bkaprt.com/icu44/02-04).

VR content crosses a new threshold because it presents fully realized experiences to people in the comfort of their own homes. But VR, of course, isn't like AR, where we can stand on the shoulders of our real-world surroundings. VR requires us to invent not only the content that will reside in a virtual space, but also the virtual space itself, whether that entails a single room or an alien world.

For the first time, though, VR technology has advanced to the point where designers without engineering backgrounds can get involved too. Today, emerging low-code and no-code tools allow designers to sketch and create their own fully fledged VR

FIG 2.9: A colleague using a VR headset to navigate a virtual space in a screenshot from an Acquia Labs video we produced.

worlds without complex code or graduate-level coursework in math. And because the underlying gadgetry is now more settled and stable, we can focus more intently on the content itself, as Jason Jerald writes in *The VR Book: Human-Centered Design for Virtual Reality* (https://bkaprt.com/icu44/02-05). Nonetheless, there are key concepts that XR designers need to know to be successful, even if they aren't diving deeply into the hardware and arithmetic.

FROM HUMAN VISION TO HEADSET VISION

VR is tough. Sure, the heavy lifting of converting human vision into mechanics that VR headsets can enable is done for us. But VR obligates us to consider how those same headsets can present information as ergonomically for the user as possible. That means showing content in virtual spaces using paradigms that are both comfortable and legible in headset vision.

As such, there are a few crucial physical concepts to understand about designing for VR:

- Field of view
- Degrees of freedom
- Content zones
- VR locomotion

Some of these concepts, namely field of view and degrees of freedom, are both integral to how we experience the world to begin with and translate the organics of human vision into the mechanics of headset vision. Others are critical for making content in VR experiences more ergonomic and useful, especially because headsets often serve as all-encompassing portals into impossible worlds bearing no resemblance to our own. Most importantly, they unlock ways for us to think about how to make content more comfortable for headset users and design with headset limitations in mind, but that doesn't mean they aren't just as instructive when we work with other types of immersive content.

Field of view

The range of what we can make out in human sight lies at the root of all visual immersive experiences. *Field of view* (FOV) encompasses everything that's visible to a user at any given time. FOV can refer to both our naturally available visual field—the peripheral range of visible space we can make out when we train our eyes on something—and the artificially manufactured field of device sensors. Whether we're talking about our own eyes, a smartphone camera, or a VR headset, FOV dictates how much immersive content we can interact with at any given time.

The human eye has an FOV of 135°; two human eyes, with overlapping FOVs, have a total FOV of 220°. So at any given moment, we can see about 60 percent of what surrounds us in a big flat circle. Due to the inherent limitations of VR technology, which at present can't encompass the full field of vision most humans naturally have, VR headset FOVs are more limited, ranging between 90° and 150°. This means that as designers, we need to acknowledge that headset users, for now, tend to have more limited leeway in what they can see as compared to their normal vision—full-screen, not widescreen. That impacts

3DoF

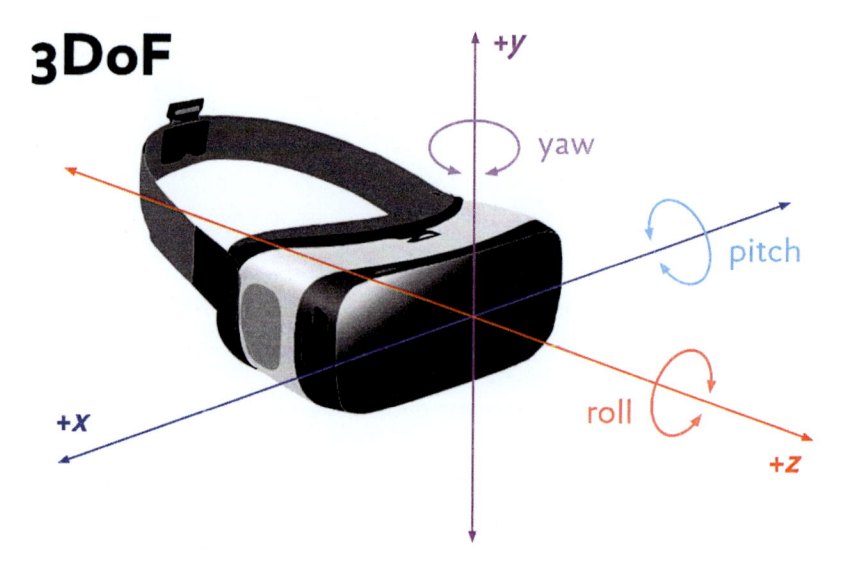

FIG 2.10: Rotational movement occurs along the three degrees of freedom (3DoF): pitch (pivoting on the *x* axis), yaw (pivoting on the *y* axis), and roll (along the *z* axis).

where we position content: not outside the ranges of all possible FOVs within a space.

Degrees of freedom

Looking in front of us, we have a static field of vision. But how do we change what shows up in our FOV? That's where moving comes into play—engaging in movements that modulate our position or orientation. All VR headsets have *three degrees of freedom* (3DoF) along which the following *rotational* movements can occur (**FIG 2.10**):

- *Pitch* is movement that occurs by looking up and down. The user's head pivots on the *x* axis, which extends horizontally across the FOV.
- *Yaw* is movement that occurs by looking left and right. The user's head pivots on the *y* axis, which extends vertically across the FOV.

6DoF

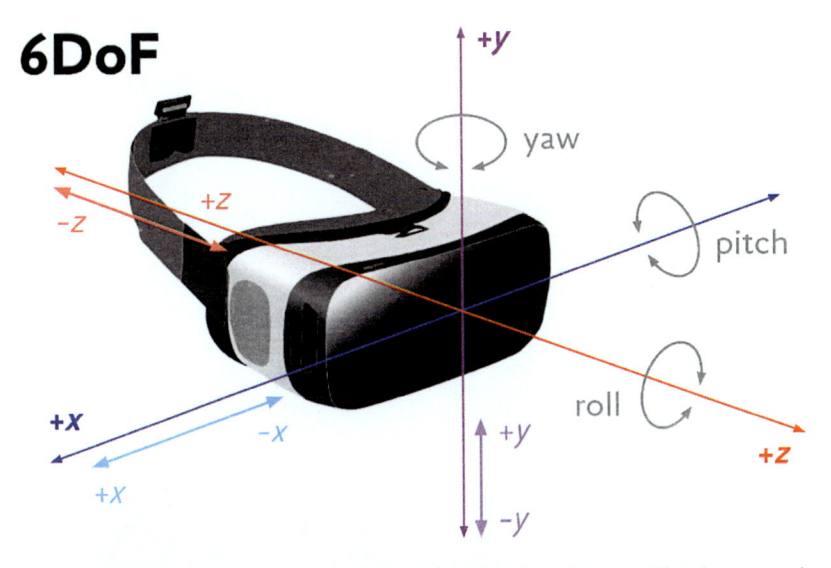

FIG 2.11: Translational movement occurs along the other three degrees of freedom to total six (6DoF): movement along the *x* axis, movement along the *y* axis, and movement along the *z* axis.

- *Roll* is movement that occurs by tilting left and right. The user's head pivots on the *z* axis, which extends forward into the FOV and onward into the horizon.

Simply put, 3DoF means that we can turn our heads any which way to modify our perspective, but that view represents only subsets of everything we can see while standing in that single, unmoving spot.

Today's headsets, because they enable navigation through changes of position and displacement, enable *six degrees of freedom* (6DoF), which entails *translational* movement (forward and reverse, left and right, and up and down) through space (**FIG 2.11**). In 6DoF-enabled headsets, you can move along the three axes translationally, not just pivot along them rotationally.

In other words, 6DoF allows us to change not just our orientation but our position as well. In 3DoF, we can't see a cat hiding directly behind a cardboard box in front of us. No matter how we change our orientation when we tilt or rotate our head or crane our neck to the side, the cat's invisible. In 6DoF, we can shuffle our feet left, right, or straight ahead to reveal the cat shrouded behind the box. We translate our entire position, not just our orientation.

It's important to understand the distinction between 3DoF and 6DoF because it has a significant impact on how we consume content in headsets. If the headset you plan to support only enables 3DoF, you'll have to take special care not to veil content behind obstacles the user can't see simply by moving their head. On the flip side, although 6DoF introduces changes in position that allow the user to see much more, it also introduces more complexity to the design; looking around while standing still is much simpler than looking around *and* moving around at the same time. If the user can't see or move past obstacles, any information lurking behind might as well not exist at all.

CONTENT ZONES

The terms *FOV* and *DoF* help us understand what human eyes and VR headsets are capable of and what's fundamentally ergonomic for both tools. But we also need to grasp the most ergonomic ways to situate content within a given FOV and how to design an immersive experience such that we don't force users to go to uncomfortable extremes along certain DoF. FOV and DoF objectively and quantitatively tell us a lot about how to save users from shooting neck pain, but they don't tell us much subjectively and qualitatively about where to look beyond those simple bounds. Now, we need to consider not just where users *can* look, but also where users *like* to look.

Based on his research at Google and previous investigation by Alex Chu at Samsung, VR technologist Mike Alger proposed the idea of *content zones* for virtual reality. Content zones describe where to situate VR content for maximum comfort and usability in terms of perceived distance (**FIG 2.12**). But they can be sources of insight for all immersive experiences

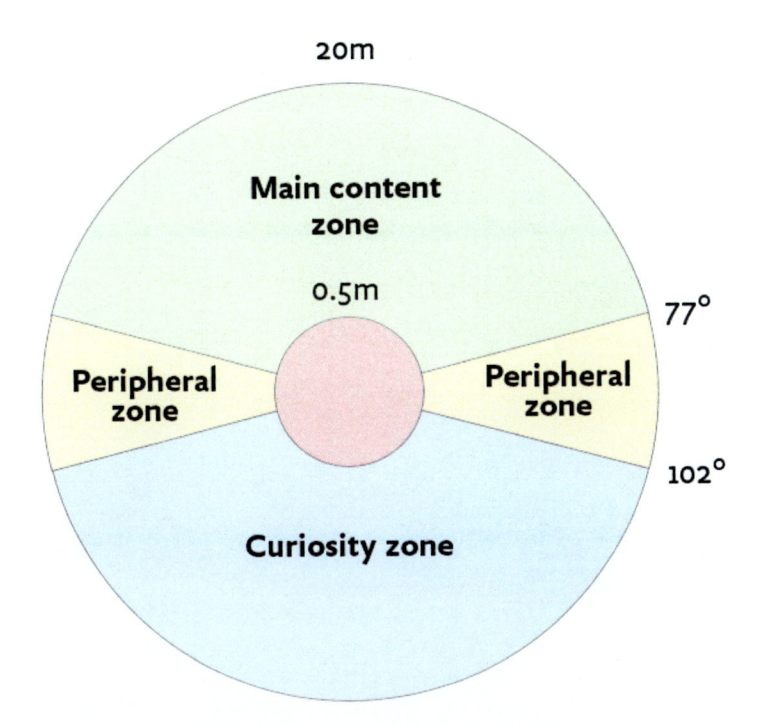

FIG 2.12: Mike Alger's content zones for virtual reality, based on his and Alex Chu's research about comfortable and maximum ranges for the placement of VR content.

---

that steep users in unfamiliar spaces, not just virtual reality. Alger recommends:

- Position important content in the *main content zone* (within ±85° left or right, +75° up, and -67° down)—anything we want to make sure the user sees or interacts with. The main content zone also includes the "Goldilocks zone" of perceived distance between 0.5 meters, which feels too close to the user's face (but might be appropriate for persistent controls or menus), and 20 meters, which feels too far.
- The *no-no zone* is anything users can see within half a meter of where they're standing, which feels too close-up to comfortably train their eyes on.

- The *peripheral zones* are only visible within our peripheral FOV and should not house any essential content, since focusing on that content requires the user to turn their head.
- The *curiosity zone* requires users to rotate their heads downward or to turn their bodies to extreme angles. This is why it's known as the "curiosity zone"—only content that justifies such a motion should be relegated to the curiosity zone, whether that means it's lower-priority or it's more of a side quest in the grand scheme of things (https://bkaprt.com/icu44/02-06).

VR LOCOMOTION

Content zones tell us where to look within a given 3DoF-enabled FOV, but how do we move through the virtual space within a given 6DoF-enabled FOV? After all, a virtual world could be immense, and we have to figure out a way to engage in locomotion without running into real-world obstacles or inadvertently injuring ourselves.

Though there are forms of VR navigation that allow us to use traditional means of locomotion—such as *omnidirectional treadmills*, on which users remain stationary in the real world while "moving" to discrete locations in a virtual world—these are costly, and typically inaccessible for wheelchair users and those using other mobility aids.

But human self-transport and vehicle-aided locomotion aren't the only kinds of mobility made possible in VR worlds. There's also the ability to travel using *artificial locomotion*, like instantly careening through interstellar space or crossing entire continents at the flick of a joystick. After all, one of the things that makes VR so attractive is that it gives users the amazing ability to travel at much higher speeds or for much longer distances than could be feasible in real life—there are no worldly limitations, after all, for a hypothetical "warp speed" in VR spaceships.

Designers leverage a slew of input methods to realize imaginary physical locomotion. As Tony Parisi wrote in *Learning Virtual Reality*, "there is currently no one standard way to interact, no 'mouse of virtual reality,' if you will." Virtual environments can be navigated through keyboards, computer mice, video game controllers, and joysticks. Many VR headsets also provide handheld touch controllers that not only track a user's gestures and interactions, but also enable flexible movement around a virtual world.

But there's a downside to many of these input methods: they often require fine motor skills and the use of both hands, making them inaccessible to many disabled users. That's why it's so crucial to offer multiple and flexible input methods, including one-handed gestures, eye-tracking, and facial gestures. This not only allows everyone to transition easily from human vision to the FOV and DoF of headset vision; it also empowers people to experience the full breadth of your immersive content comfortably via content zones and artificial locomotion.

IMMERSION IS A CONTINUUM

Immersion isn't just about fancy VR fantasias that conjure complicated visual effects, or impressive machine vision capabilities that summon AR overlays. Nor is it solely about how we carve up screens for digital signage or FOVs for headsets, or where we position beacons for locational content. We've purposefully taken a broad look at the idea of immersive content in this book because immersion is highly subjective, and not rooted in a specific present-day technology.

No matter the underlying gadgetry, we need to focus on users and their needs, striving always to offer better ways to access and interact with content. If an edict comes from higher-ups to "do metaverse content" or "do something with AR," it might be time to run for the hills, because immersive content is first and foremost about real humans. But for many organizations, most content isn't ready for orbit because it's tethered to websites. How do we move it beyond the strictures of the screen?

3 CONTENT IMMERSION

IN RECENT YEARS, content has undergone single channel-to-channel paradigm shifts—from print to web, from web to mobile—but we're increasingly seeing a vast array of berths where content can end up: web, mobile, tablet, Braille displays, voice interfaces, extended reality, digital signage, and more still over the horizon.

But screens still define most of the content we ingest daily, whether it's something we absorb on a smartphone, computer, or television. We've defined immersive content as a new state—content freed from its boxed-in trappings and imbued with a sense of place. So that means all we have to do is forklift our existing web, mobile, and TV content into an immersive experience, right? Wrong. Immersive content demands we treat the space it lands in as its ideal habitat.

For many organizations, the primary challenge of immersive content isn't merely conceiving copy for spatial experiences, but rather juggling it alongside other channels for content delivery. While some teams might have the ability to disburse all that channel-specific content separately, many of us have to recycle the same content in multiple ways to keep things manageable. Organizations crafting a content strategy now need to anticipate ahead of time, not react to after the fact, all the conceivable places where our copy and media could end up—especially channels and spaces that might not even exist yet.

After all, many of us working on digital content have primarily focused on websites, where there are probably more than a few skeletons in the closet and spider-filled nooks and crannies where copy is egregiously out of date or hilariously ill-suited for the immersive medium. I don't just mean text that hasn't seen an editor's touch since 2002; I also mean content using context-heavy references like "on this same page" and "below this paragraph" or channel-specific directions like "read more" and "download PDF," all fossils that can confound those who are accessing our copy solely through immersive means. These problems prevent our content from being truly multimodal.

Now, we need to run our existing copy through a new gauntlet: Does it honor its form and function in space, respecting the unique needs of locational devices, digital signs, and VR headsets while keeping in mind the larger demands of our omnichannel world? As designers, we need to call upon a slew of new processes: writing good immersive content and reusing existing content in immersive ways, and especially auditing content for its immersive readiness.

WHAT MOVES YOUR USERS?

First things first: don't pigeonhole website copy into a VR headset or digital sign simply because some newfangled immersive technology now makes it possible. Instead, decide on the right mix of delivery approaches for your users—whether that's a single digital sign or multiple immersive channels—by considering how immersive content fits into your larger content strategy and how your users will interact with it to derive value.

Immerse yourself in the problem

Though our mission should always be to do what's best for our users, designers often contend with stakeholders and executives hell-bent on financial outcomes and marketing fodder that may have little to do with the actual problem that customers face. While this might make business sense, ultimately, your immersive content should be motivated, and its existence justified, by what problem or nuisance drives your users. For this reason, before anything else, it's best to:

- **Do user research.** Chances are you've already got a space you're working with, whether it's a shopping mall, a train station, or a virtual environment. As you would with any other design process, first strive to understand the user and how they interact with your existing interfaces (like websites and mobile apps) and physical spaces. Interview a broad range of users who spend time in both the spatial environments and the digital interfaces they regularly encounter to probe the problem space. What are their pain points and objectives in both settings? Where is there overlap?
- **Write a problem statement.** This one's easier said than done. Without landing on a clear problem statement that captures pain points, your audience won't ever come back. Aim for a single sentence and avoid "solutioneering," where you presuppose the user wants a particular answer rather than focusing first and foremost on their issues. One way to do this is to write a user story, along these lines: "As a subway commuter on a platform, I need to know when the next train is arriving and what alternate routes I can take if it's delayed."
- **Define measurable success.** What's the goal of your organization and how does it dovetail with your user's own goals? Is it to get your customers to spend more time or money in your AR-enabled brick-and-mortar store? Is it to deliver crucial information as efficiently as possible through push notifications so users can make split-second decisions? Whether your organization defines success as foot traffic or web traffic, recurring revenue or response rates, having specific and well-defined criteria for success will buttress the business value of your immersive content.
- What motivates your users, and what content are they looking for? Everything else comes second.

Focus on the user, not the device

So you've clearly identified the right mix of motivations for your immersive content, rooted in a well-investigated problem statement and measurable success. Now you need to start asking questions. The following queries can help you and your team get the most out of an immersive content implementation without overly biasing your solution toward a particular technology:

- **What sort of content, and how much of it, do your users need?** What's the word count and the optimal "size" for a minimum viable piece of immersive content, a single *content item*? Are your users' needs met by chunkier macrocontent or by more granular microcontent? Do they need only a smidgen of copy, or do they need much longer tracts of information to acquire what they need?
- **How much time do your users have?** Do your users have the luxury of stopping to read for a moment without disrupting traffic, or do they have but mere seconds to glance at some copy before making an on-the-spot decision?
- **Do your users need embedded content or environmental content?** Are your users averse to turning on location services on their phone, and would they be more amenable to a digital sign helping them navigate a space instead? Do your users prefer to do their in-store browsing at home in the comfort of a wearable headset or in the flesh with AR overlays hovering over products in their hand? Or both?

Only once you know what your users need should you answer the final question in the list. Usually, by this time, the answers will have already illuminated a clear path forward.

Gravitate toward progressive disclosure

Think about the best-designed web, mobile, and voice apps you've come across. The best, or at least the most efficient, don't overwhelm you with too much choice or too much chatter. They give you just what you need and nothing more, unless you veer from the well-trodden path into a land of exception. In websites, this shows up as registration or setup wizards. In mobile apps, in onboarding flows. In voice interfaces, in increasingly long-winded and detailed prompts.

Space is no different. Grand transit hubs are designed with the most common "happy path" in mind for the traveler, shepherding them to their desired track with the minimum amount of friction possible. That's because we humans have a limited capacity for decision-making. Why shower a commuter with irrelevant signage when chances are they're only deviating by a little from the default path all transit users are taking? From airports to art museums, we see large, hulking, well-trodden paths give way to smaller rivulets in ways that mirror how we show people ever narrower, more specific information relevant to what, precisely, they want.

This all-too-common phenomenon has a name. In *progressive disclosure*, wherever possible, we surface the most essential information first and defer less pertinent material to surface farther along the journey. Are there opportunities to allow the user to tap through to a more exhaustive overview or website—i.e., linked content—if they have the time to stay awhile, instead of presenting all advice in one fell swoop? What's a summary-sized version of your content that can be expressed as a single content item, such as a push notification or VR overlay, while the rest is relegated to a linked page or view?

Fortunately, immersive content in many regards is simply an extension of much of the spatially rooted analog content we consume daily: signage, in physical environments like corporate buildings and department stores; and labeling, on products on shelves and next to artifacts in museums. So, how do we write it?

READABLE AND REACHABLE

Like any other content, good immersive content is both legible and discoverable. Our job isn't just to extend device-bound content into built or virtual environments; it's to ensure content can be accessed, understood, and used, no matter the user's surroundings. Is your content accessible, reachable, and in an appropriate setting for its purpose? Will it be positioned near other copy that may outshine or interfere with it? And is it something that users won't necessarily need to wait a long time to discover?

Legibility

What does it mean for immersive content to be *legible*? For embedded content, legibility is, to some extent, literally about the ability to parse text on a given device, whether that entails SMS messages or AR overlays. The legibility of environmental content, however, is more nuanced due to its inherent unpredictability. Rather than leaning on device capabilities as a foundation, we have to think like signage illustrators and interior designers.

In both the embedded and environmental cases, users are seldom focused on a single device, because their attention is also partially devoted to their surroundings, like an unfamiliar airport or college campus, for instance. How quickly can users in motion read, and internalize, the information they need?

Designers must consider whether the user will have enough context to understand the content in that moment; whether the content is the appropriate length for its space; and whether color, typography, and other elements make the content more visible.

Context: Does it make sense?

In web and print content, we've long had the benefit of context being scoped to the borders of the visible screen or the printable page. We can refer to previous paragraphs or pages at will, without feeling marooned. But now that our perspective spans our physical surroundings *in addition to* our screens and devices, our notion of context has to expand, too. Context can now entail not only abstract locational references to "on the previous page" or "earlier in this paragraph," but also concrete spatial ones like "at the previous stop" or "right behind you."

With embedded content, the user has to switch their operating context between a device screen and the world around them. A smartphone alert about a stalled subway train, for instance, immediately removes them from the confines of that device and pushes them to reorient themselves to the larger scope of the transit system. The context of their experience shifts from a handheld device to the upcoming transfer station, where they may decide to switch lines to accelerate their commute.

In the case of environmental content, the context is fixed to the user's surroundings rather than limited to a smartphone screen. Locational references like "four stops ahead" and iconography such as arrows make far more sense when a commuter is moving through the physical environment of a subway station than when they're reading an alert on their smartphone.

Sometimes, though, context-switching is unavoidable; many experiences need to mix embedded and environmental content. After all, handheld devices can provide much more valuable insight or more personalized information than digital signs for the general public could ever muster.

When the user finds themselves juggling their device-bound frame of reference and the world around them, we shouldn't toss in another ball for them to juggle. Any ancillary content that lies at the narrower ends of progressive disclosure—the distant browser page with extra information, the "read more" detail that unfurls into a new app screen—should lie well within their device's borders, a manageable scope. We should strive to limit context-switching to only the two realms the user is already contending with: the physical space they're navigating and the device they hold in their hands.

But this complicates our effort to make all immersive content legible. After all, movements (changes in position or orientation) are how we modify our physical context, but there are other changes, like in-channel shifts (context switches within the same interface) and cross-channel shifts (context switches across digital channels) to account for. Consider, for instance, user movements occurring not in physical space but within a device, from a locational push notification to a relevant website or from a VR overlay to a built-in browser with more information (FIG 3.1).

Embedded content — **Environmental content**

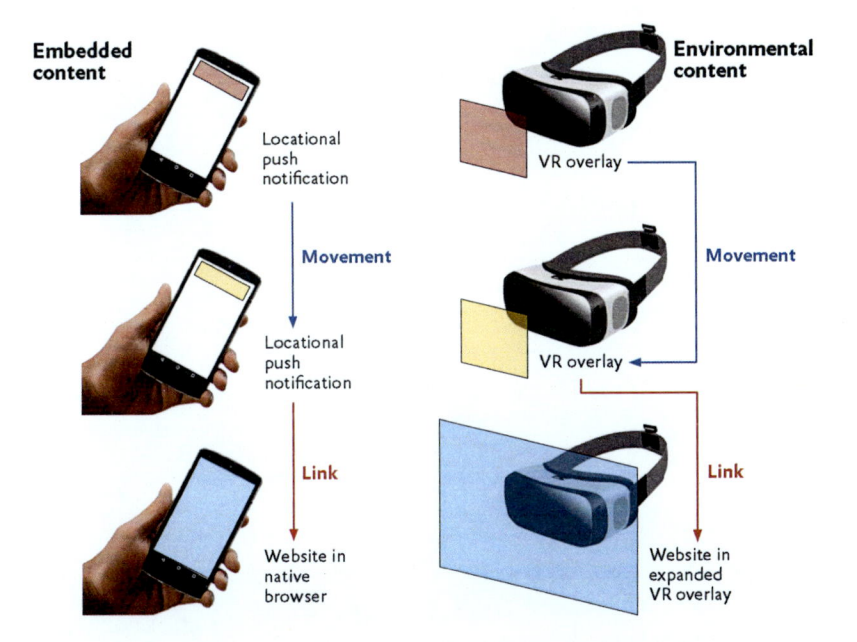

- Locational push notification → Movement → Locational push notification → Link → Website in native browser
- VR overlay → Movement → VR overlay → Link → Website in expanded VR overlay

FIG 3.1: Our context can change based on movement (change in position or orientation) or based on following a link to linked content (by clicking or otherwise interacting with a call to action).

Since context changes can occur across movements, parts of an interface, or entire channels, we have to be especially careful about *phantom references*, which are pointers to areas a user can't access in the given moment. Consider, for instance, an unfollowable link like "click here" or "learn more," which is likely to fail silently, or a parenthetical about a PDF available for download in a VR headset, an aside that isn't very useful since headsets aren't a great way to open PDFs.

Verbosity: Is the content the right length?

Immersive content can run the gamut from relentlessly wordy to emptily wordless. Consider two signs on a subway platform that announce a disruption to service: one goes on and on,

FIG 3.2: This analog sign conveys a service disruption with high verbosity and was posted on a subway platform before the disruption began, warning commuters ahead of time.

FIG 3.3: This analog sign conveys a service disruption with less verbosity and was posted outside a subway station after the disruption began, warning commuters in the moment.

offering detailed information about alternate routes for commuters who need it (**FIG 3.2**), while the other is succinct, hastily scribbled, and demands no more than a quick glance (**FIG 3.3**). These represent two extremes of the verbosity spectrum.

Because embedded content relies on some encircling device, like a smartphone or tablet, the way it relates to the physical space around it should determine the length of the content. A subway commuter in motion is often grateful for a quick push notification that tersely tracks an ongoing delay, but if they could sit down on a bench and tap that notification, they might be more open to a longer explanation of the underlying issue, or a list of alternate routes they could take instead, allowing them to better plan their trip into work.

IMMERSIVE CONTENT AND USABILITY

Environmental content works in much the same way. Most digital signage is geared toward travelers looking for the most efficient possible way to get from point *A* to point *B*. But if your digital signage allows for touch interaction, as with a touchscreen information kiosk in an airport or a scrollable store directory in a shopping mall, a little length can go a long way. In VR gaming, a player pursued by a zombie will want mission-critical content presented as quickly as possible, whereas a player exploring an open-world video game expects more leisurely reading or even a chance to microwave some popcorn, like experiencing the journal entries in the classic *Myst computer game series*.

Ultimately, if the user is in a hurry, keep it short. If they can stop and browse for a while, lengthier copy can and should be available to them.

Visibility: Can I see it?

Visibility can be a pesky problem for both embedded and environmental content. For embedded content, we may need to consult material on our device screens while our eyes dart around, glancing at other things in our FOV. For environmental content, which is necessarily part and parcel of our surroundings and subject to the whims of lighting conditions and awkward angles, visibility is an even more nuanced concern.

Web content has the privilege of being read when users aren't moving. On the other hand, immersive content is often *intended* to be consumed while we're in motion rather than standing still and on a stationary device in isolation. That makes the following considerations all the more critical for immersive content design:

- **Typography.** Your choice of typeface, font size, and text style all have an outsized impact on your content's legibility and readability in a variety of scenarios (**FIG 3.4**). Many digital signs use sans serif typefaces and all caps for text. Does it make sense to follow in those footsteps or not? Consider how various users will read your content. If you allow users to increase text size or change the font as they see fit,

FIG 3.4: The rightmost screen in this digital signage at San Francisco International Airport displays speech-to-text captions for important airport announcements (in this case, about the facility's mask mandate), but it's difficult to read from a distance.

even better; for instance, some dyslexics may find fonts like OpenDyslexic, Arial, and Comic Sans more readable than other common choices (https://bkaprt.com/icu44/03-01).
- **Color.** A color scheme without sufficient contrast will render your content unreadable, especially for people with low vision or color blindness. From a distance, a high-contrast palette—light text on a dark background—is critical for those who may only have a second to absorb what you have to say. Any semitransparent AR overlays should be opaque enough to read, whether they're embedded on a device or environmentally exposed in a VR headset (FIG 3.5).
- **Lighting.** Consider how your information will display in well lit, poorly lit, or, in the case of VR, artificially lit situations. Does glare from surrounding lighting render your content invisible, whether it's embedded on a device or displaying on a wall (FIG 3.6)? Does overly ambient darkness require a user to brighten their device's screen to read?

FIG 3.5: The overlay in this AR prototype is opaque enough for the text to be easily read over the image.

- **Perspective.** Some people may be too tall or too short to read a digital sign comfortably, while others may be unable to crane their necks or rotate their heads too far. Users of digital signs and VR headsets need to be able to make out content at a variety of angles, none of which might be optimal.
- **Accessible display.** If you're suspending a digital sign in a building or summoning an AR overlay in a smartphone, is there text-to-speech audio captioning available for Blind users? Can users connect a refreshable Braille display to acquire the same information? In the case of physical spaces, are there clear cues that convey alternatives to any messages, such as tactile paving (**FIG 3.7**)? Is your embedded content compatible with the device's native screen reader?

FIG 3.6: Some text displayed on this digital sign at the Dekalb Avenue station in the New York City Subway may be rendered illegible due to glare from overhead lighting on the upper half of the sign; screen damage in the lower half also interferes.

FIG 3.7: In the built environment, truncated domes are tactile indicators that assist Blind and low-vision pedestrians underfoot as they travel on streets and transit platforms. Photograph by Richard Drdul (CC-BY-SA-2.0, https://bkaprt.com/icu44/03-02).

Visibility isn't just a matter of sign placement or text size. It's also about the ability for all people to consume the same content, no matter what disabilities they may have. This means considering not just visibility, but also audibility and, in some cases, tactility. While physical accessibility is now commonplace in many urban centers (after a monumental amount of activism), most places still lack audio captioning or raised Braille dots for critical information conveyed in space.

Discoverability

We can perfect the readability of our content, but none of that matters if users can't find that content in the first place, especially when potentially labyrinthine spaces are involved. A change in a user's position or orientation may trigger all manner of events, like machine vision detecting a new item in a grocery store, or a digital sign coming into view as the user crosses an airport threshold. With immersive content, discoverability depends on access, proximity, and timing.

Access: Is it easy to get?

Access isn't merely about the reachability and ideal setting of your content; it's also about ensuring that everyone, especially disabled people, can discover the information we want to deliver in the spaces they're in without too much work. Unfortunately, immersive content is all too easy to silo by preventing users from getting to it altogether.

Make sure that the places where content should appear are in areas where users can find them. With embedded content, that means asking questions like:

- Is each content item clearly associated with a specific point or range in space? As an example, a wayward page of content set adrift without any clear tether to a particular place isn't immersive-ready.
- Is each content item accessible to all? For instance, copy tied to a beacon at the top of a staircase means that wheelchair users won't see it.

- Are content items spaced at reasonable distances? For example, product copy in an AR overlay far away from other, more densely packed-together products will be harder for users to find.

In environmental situations:

- Can the content be found in the environment? For instance, you don't want to place a digital sign behind a wall too cumbersome to go around. Make sure people will come across signage in their natural movements through a space. For VR worlds, it's important to design the environment carefully so each sign or overlay is discoverable; narrow passages and cut-off rooms are particularly problematic.
- Can the content show up in its full glory without anything else stealing the limelight? For instance, a VR overlay might appear over an important other element in a virtual setting, like the description of an orchid in a virtual botanical garden covering up too much of the specimen it's supposed to identify.
- This last bullet point brings us to another issue: What happens when you have two overlays popping up too close to each other, something asking this last question won't fix?

Proximity: Does it overlap?

Whereas access is a yes-or-no question, *proximity* has to do with a content item's spatial relationship to other content. Because immersive experiences require us to position content in a space, it's easy for a piece of content to collide with other pieces of content.

With embedded content, such overlap can lead to confusion. Beacons positioned too closely together can lead to scenarios where a user receives multiple conflicting pieces of information at the same time (**FIG 3.8**). For example, they could receive two push notifications simultaneously because they're standing on the threshold between two airline gates, or between two departments in a store. By the same token, with environmental content, digital signs too closely positioned to each other

User location

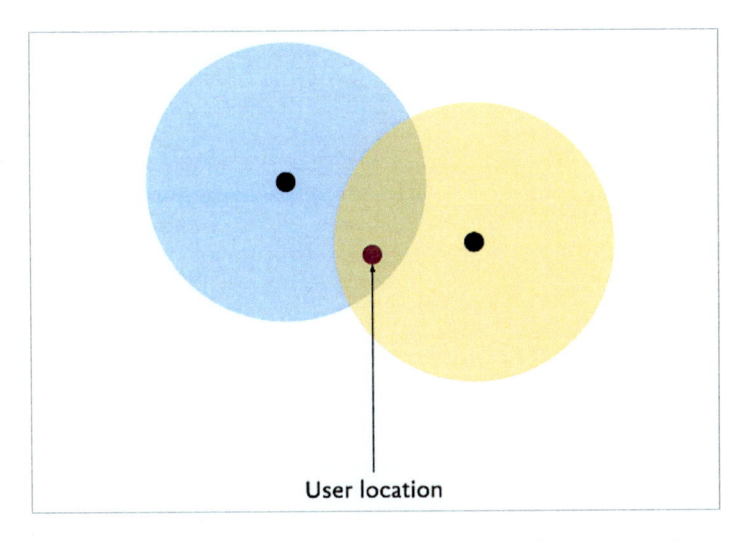

FIG 3.8: When two beacon ranges overlap, potentially conflicting content items are delivered at the same time to the user's present location.

might surface ambiguity in users' minds about which content has higher priority.

In XR content, overlapping overlays or displays (**FIG 3.9**) can not only lead to some content becoming inaccessible, but can also potentially induce seizures in people with epilepsy when multiple pieces of content quickly flash in and out of view.

Drawing storyboards, interaction flow diagrams, and spatial maps, as we'll see in Chapter 4, can help avoid some of these pitfalls, though these types of flaws are often only detected through copious iterative testing.

Timing: When is it there?

One of the chief challenges of immersive content is how much of it to display and when. With web design, we've learned that timed carousels and slideshows frustrate users and ultimately render content undiscoverable (https://bkaprt.com/icu44/03-03). For most immersive content, the same principle holds true. *Timing* in immersive content means coming across information

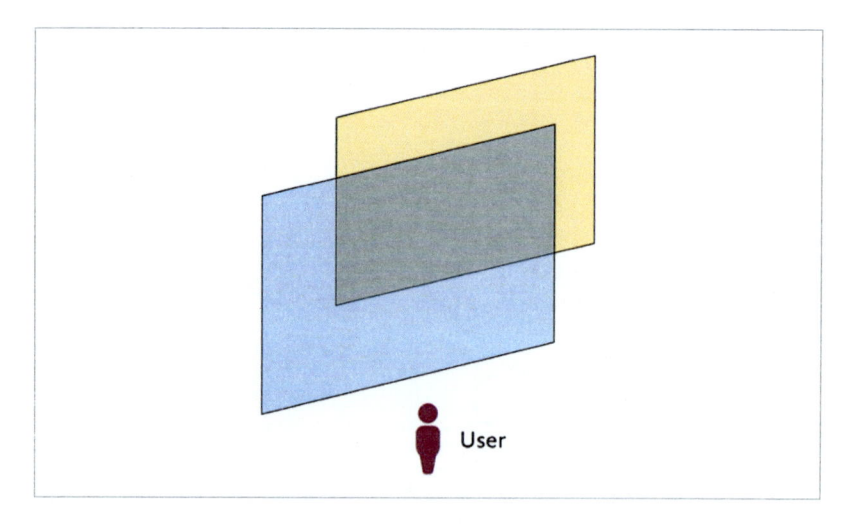

FIG 3.9: Overlapping semitransparent XR overlays can impact the legibility and discoverability of both as the user views the space through an XR headset.

at just the right time, not just in the right perceptual circumstances. How long must users wait for essential content?

Depending on when a user comes across a piece of immersive content, the content they need most might require a delay, or it might require them to have context established by prior content that's no longer available in that moment. For instance, a passenger coming across a digital sign in the New York City Subway may have to wait for a long message to finish scrolling (**FIG 3.10**), or for it to repeat because they came across it too late. Granted, in the case of the latter, this sort of poor timing is often unavoidable, especially given extenuating circumstances like emergency notifications, or lucrative advertisements that overtake the entire screen, shoving aside other critical information at just the wrong instant.

FIG 3.10: This digital sign from the 30th Avenue station in the New York City Subway shows a ticker in the bottom right corner stating, "Please stand back from the platform edge." Depending on when the user comes across the sign, the message may not be readable until the next slow repetition of the ticker begins.

NOW BOARDING: NEW CONTENT FOR AN AIRPORT

In 2017, I began exploring immersive content professionally at Acquia with my colleagues Chris Hamper, Alena "ASH" Heath, and Drew Robertson. In our airline passenger case study, we wanted to solve a common challenge: how to improve the customer experience of a traveler navigating an unfamiliar airport (https://bkaprt.com/icu44/03-04, video).

We conducted user research to uncover some of the ways passengers expect airline apps to supply information at key moments in their journeys, as well as the major frictions flyers experience at a new airport. For instance, though many aircrews announce on landing at which baggage carousel checked luggage will be available, people are prone to let that knowledge slip from memory. In addition, we found many people,

CONTENT IMMERSION 53

especially infrequent flyers, find first-time visits to new airports intimidating, and may not know where to find the baggage-claim area in the first place, especially given carousels are often shared between carriers.

Much of this info, of course, is available on airline websites. For instance, the "Airport Maps & Locations" page of Delta Air Lines' website contains a zoomable graphic of its route network (FIG 3.11) and generic details about security and baggage policies (FIG 3.12). But it's an experience more conducive to browsing on a computer at home as helpful prep for a trip, or on a phone while waiting to board at a gate. It isn't necessarily the most efficient guide for a user arriving at a new airport for the first time who feels very lost.

A great deal of the content we find on airline websites isn't all that helpful for a user in motion without the luxury of time or willingness to sift through it. The mission of our case study, in that vein, was to deliver content to users in the context of their handheld device—embedded in their smartphones—without in any way blocking their journey to their destination.

That could mean single-channel content limited to the mobile app itself, or cross-channel content spread across digital signs and a mobile app accessed at will. After all, a passenger might prefer to confirm a gate change on a digital departure board even after receiving a push notification about it on an app. Rather than scrollable, long-form content plastered across pages, we would need one-stop, short-form content arranged into tightly written push notifications at certain points along their route.

To help the user along quickly, whether their journey was from their arrival gate to a baggage-claim carousel or from the drop-off lane to a departing gate, we decided to prototype an immersive experience within a fictitious airline's mobile app that would include helpful content (https://bkaprt.com/icu44/03-04, video).

Identifying individual airport journeys

We explored two distinct user journeys: one for checking in and heading to a departure gate, and another to guide the user to

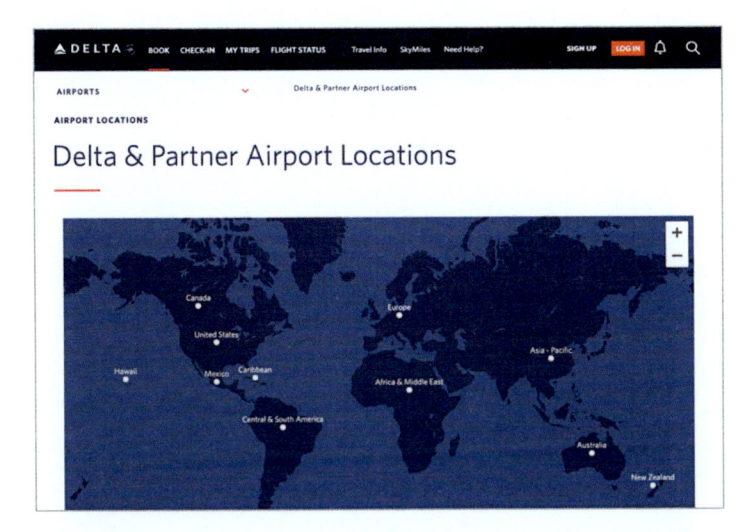

FIG 3.11: The Delta Air Lines website's "Airport Maps & Locations" page displays a map of its route network across the world, but, as of this writing, accessing an individual airport's information requires multiple successive clicks or taps, which isn't very efficient for passengers in a rush (https://bkaprt.com/icu44/03-05).

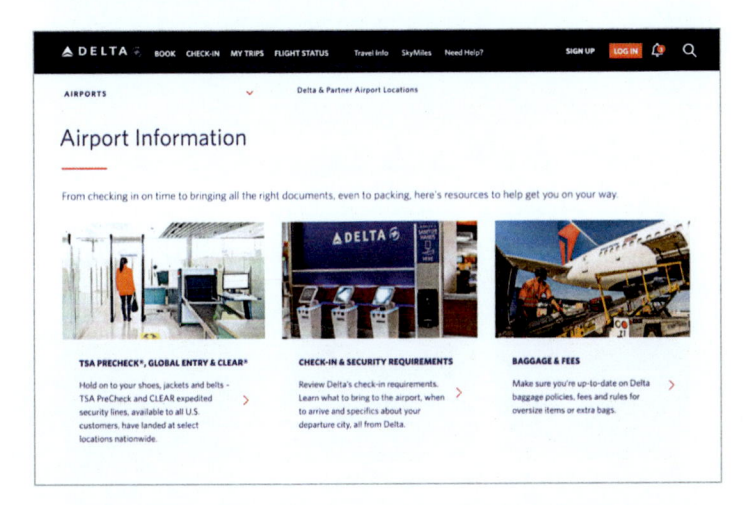

FIG 3.12: The Delta Air Lines website's "Airport Maps & Locations" page includes generic information about security protocols, check-in requirements, and baggage policies—but this applies to every airport across the carrier's network, not the individual airport at which someone has just landed (https://bkaprt.com/icu44/03-05).

CONTENT IMMERSION   55

Departure from airport

| Entrance to terminal departures area | → | Check-in kiosk | → | Security checkpoint | → | Departure gate |

FIG 3.13: A diagram depicting the journey our airline passenger undertakes when departing from an unfamiliar airport.

---

the assigned baggage-claim carousel if they had a checked bag. At key touchpoints in the user journeys, we wanted to ensure that the user would receive key content about their departure or arrival, paired with airport maps containing live wayfinding to show them the route. Though we could certainly branch out with links to still more information, such as a push notification that invites the user to "read more" on a page from the airline website, the content we were most interested in was the sort that keeps the user moving rather than stopping them cold.

Let's first look at an airline passenger's journey when departing from a new airport (**FIG 3.13**). In our case study, upon arrival at the airport, the app pings the user with a push notification:

> **Departure welcome message:** Welcome to Terminal 2 at John F. Kennedy International Airport. Your flight, Delta 5410, is scheduled to depart from Gate C66 at 5:01 p.m.
>
> See interactive map | Visit website

After checking their bag, they receive another notification:

> **Check-in message:** Your checked bag number is 02288299812.

Once they've proceeded through the security checkpoint, they receive the following:

> **Airside message:** Your flight, Delta 5410, is scheduled to depart from Gate C66 at 5:01 p.m. Boarding begins in 26 minutes at 4:26 p.m. and ends 15 minutes before departure.
>
> See interactive map | Visit website

Arrival at airport

Arrival gate → Exit to terminal arrivals area → Baggage claim carousel

FIG 3.14: A diagram depicting the journey our airline passenger undertakes when arriving at an unfamiliar airport.

Finally, at the departure gate, they receive:

Predeparture message: *You've arrived at Gate C66. Boarding for your flight, Delta 5410, begins in 15 minutes at 4:26 p.m. and ends 15 minutes before departure.*

Visit website

What about a user who's arriving at this strange airport instead of departing from it (FIG 3.14)? Upon getting to the arrival gate, they receive the following notifications, depending on whether they've checked a bag previously or not:

Welcome message (with checked bag): *Welcome to Terminal 2 at John F. Kennedy International Airport. You're currently at Gate C68. Your checked bag 02288299812 will be available at Carousel #3.*

See interactive map | Visit website

Welcome message (without checked bag): *Welcome to Welcome to Terminal 2 at John F. Kennedy International Airport.*

See interactive map | Visit website

Once they exit to terminal arrivals area, if they checked a bag before, they receive a push notification:

Landside message (with checked bag): *Your checked bag 02288299812 will be available in 6 minutes at Carousel #3.*

Connecting through airport

| Arrival gate | → | Departure gate |

FIG 3.15: A diagram depicting the journey our airline passenger undertakes when arriving at an unfamiliar airport.

See interactive map | Visit website

Finally, they're notified again with a helpful message when they arrive at the correct baggage claim carousel:

Baggage claim message (with checked bag): *You've arrived at Carousel #3.*

Visit website

What if the user is simply connecting through this airport rather than departing from or arriving to it (FIG 3.15), a journey we didn't explore in our prototype? At the arrival gate, they're greeted with this push notification:

Welcome message: *Welcome to Terminal 2 at John F. Kennedy International Airport. Your connection, Delta 5410, is scheduled to depart from Gate C66 at 5:01 p.m.*

See interactive map | Visit website

And another when they've found their departure gate:

Predeparture message: *You've arrived at Gate C66. Boarding for your flight, Delta 5410, begins in 15 minutes at 4:26 p.m. and ends 15 minutes before departure.*

Visit website

What we learned in flight

A challenge of authoring good immersive content—beyond, of course, the act of writing well for physical spaces and user movement—is the balancing act between the copy we craft and the limitations of the spaces in which we operate. Without considering both, you might end up boxing your content into a been-there-done-that journey that does little to enhance the user's experience, or you could stretch your content too thin across too many touchpoints.

Our project taught us some intriguing lessons that apply to any immersive content experience. Sometimes, writing new content is necessary to honor the uniqueness of the immersive medium. Website content simply doesn't work for someone who needs immediate information tuned to where they are. And together, the push notifications pointed to a different sort of airline passenger experience: a vision not wedded to devices often forcing us to stand still, but rather a more seamless, location-aware ideal. Despite the seeming cacophony push notifications often represent, we found in our demos that they created a cohesive and harmonious journey from start to finish. It's no secret why so many airlines now have mobile apps that emulate the same strategy.

There were, of course, drawbacks to this airline passenger case study, such as privacy concerns around personalization and location tracking by beacons, and its myopic view of the possible journeys a user might need to take through an airport—after all, some passengers will inevitably deviate from these well-trodden paths. The app only unfurls a few push notifications, but if we were to extend this prototype further, we'd want to incorporate even more alerts than the ones depicted. Moreover, it would've been worth our time to ponder whether a mixed, cross-channel approach weaving together both environmental digital signage and embedded beacon-driven content could have made the user journey even more efficient.

FIG 3.16: A screenshot from the demo video of our AR prototype, demonstrating how content is reused across the supermarket's website and the immersive AR experience.

EXPRESS CHECKOUT: CONTENT REUSE AT A SUPERMARKET

Store websites and their brick-and-mortar counterparts share one big thing in common: both need to display products, and information about those products, in a way that entices the customer to make a purchase. The commonalities between these spaces offer special opportunities to examine how we can share content between existing and immersive experiences.

To investigate the potential for content reuse, I worked on a grocery shopper case study along with my Acquia Labs colleagues in 2017. Through user research, we discovered shoppers are often curious about products—in search of nutritional facts and dietary advice, for example—but feel limited by the information available on the shelves and product labels.

After some discussion, we decided to design an AR experience that would let anyone scan a grocery item through machine vision on their smartphone to unlock more in-depth content about it. It was the perfect opportunity to leverage already available content to give the user an in-store immersive experience (FIG 3.16).

We already had a lot of content related to each product thanks to the grocery store's ecommerce website. But reusing content isn't a simple matter of copying text and photos wholesale from the website and pasting them into an AR overlay. After all, screen real estate on a smartphone is sorely lacking, and we can only accommodate so much.

Consider the following product information a shopper might find on a supermarket website:

Product:	Colavita Marinara Sauce
Price:	$7.99
Rating:	3.5 (2 ratings)
Reviews:	"Pretty good!" (4 stars)
	"Basic Marinara" (3 stars)
Description:	Colavita Marinara Sauce is perfect for an intimate night in with spaghetti and meatballs and always uses the freshest ingredients (download PDF). Read more about Colavita Marinara Sauce.
Dietary information:	None

This content is great for a website as is, but how immersive-ready is it? Well, for one, is there really a need for that PDF download link? Are our app users interested in decamping from the confines of the AR experience, or do they want to shop free of distractions? In the end, we need to adjust much of our content so it's better suited for immersive contexts.

But how do we evaluate web content to know whether it's immersive-ready? For that, we need a content audit.

CONTENT IMMERSION

Immersive content audits

Content audits are common across our industry—we use them to assess how compliant our copy is with internet regulations, how accessible it is for users with various disabilities, whether it's out of date, and much more. Rarely, however, do we use content audits to assess our content's fitness across the spectrum of all conceivable digital experiences: websites, mobile apps, chatbots, voice interfaces, you name it.

In my 2021 book *Voice Content and Usability* (https://bkaprt.com/icu44/03-06), I shared how to audit website content in order to assess its readiness for a content-driven voice interface, and all of that advice still stands. The key steps are applicable for immersive content audits too:

1. **Write a questionnaire.** Create a list of questions that evaluates each piece of content based on the channel it's intended for, whether that means an AR overlay, a push notification, or a digital sign. Your questions should probe whether the content is legible or discoverable in its new habitat:
    a) **Content legibility.** Is the content legible from a variety of vantage points and perspectives, such as on digital signage or in AR overlays? Does the content have the appropriate *verbosity tolerance*, and does it avoid any *phantom references* that make your content harder to understand for users in physical spaces?
    b) **Content discoverability.** Is your content accessible from every possible point in the space? For example, is it associated with a point of interest that isn't reachable (such as a web page for a museum artwork that is critical to the user experience but not reachable due to restricted access)? Is there any potential for it to overlap or conflict with other content, and is there any way it could remain undiscovered because of a user coming across it at the wrong time?
2. **Choose your criteria.** Once you have the questions, you need to know how to judge the answers and what you'll do with them. Create *evaluation criteria* to establish a threshold beyond which action is necessary, and *recommendation crite-*

ria to prescribe what action you should take. For instance, one example of an evaluation criterion would be "Check to see if any actions are impossible to realize" (such as "reading more" or "learning more" when a user is in a VR headset). An example of a recommendation criterion in response would be to remove all calls to action that users can't complete in that context.

3. **Assess the content.** After determining the evaluation criteria and recommendation criteria, sit down with a full corpus of your content and run through it with a fine-tooth comb, imagining how it would behave in an immersive setting and applying your list of evaluation criteria against it. Finally, meet with your team, including fellow designers, technologists, and all stakeholders, to cover the results of the content audit and determine what steps to take based on the recommended actions.

This isn't a comprehensive overview of how an audit might look for your overall body of content, and this process won't be the same for each implementation. Nonetheless, content auditing is an important step that'll help your team understand how your copy will work across both immersive channels and those you might want to incorporate later. The outcome of your audit might indicate that your current copy is a nonstarter, and that you need to write some stuff from scratch, as we found in our airline passenger case study—and that's okay. But if you find that some of your content can be reused, the next step is revising.

Reworking content for immersive use

For certain immersive experiences, writing new content is essential because there isn't much copy to go off. But often better, especially if you're time- or budget-strapped as an organization, is to look for information already present in your digital properties and reuse it. "Content reuse" is a common catchphrase in omnichannel content strategy because it keeps the editorial burden manageable.

We can prepare existing website content for an immersive environment without reducing its value for users of either channel. Consider our website's marinara sauce description:

> Colavita Marinara Sauce *is perfect for an intimate night in with spaghetti and meatballs and always uses the freshest ingredients. See below for reviews.* Read more about Colavita Marinara Sauce.
>
> Reviews:
> "Pretty good!" (4/5)
> "Basic marinara" (3/5)

Certain calls to action found in web content, like web-specific "read more" links, are nonsensical, distracting, and unrealizable in non-web contexts. Links that point to other supplemental information, like a pointer to a PDF download, might not appear in the AR interface your audience sees due to a lack of link functionality available in the app, or, even worse, there might not be a way to open a PDF from the app. These are considerations you'll need to think about as you perform your content audit. For instance, let's assume that our AR app aims to limit context-switching by keeping the user within the AR experience. Let's replace this nonsensical call to action with an in-context link that makes our content still consumable by web users but limits distractions for AR users:

> Colavita Marinara Sauce *is perfect for an intimate night in with spaghetti and meatballs and always uses the freshest ingredients. See below for reviews.*
> Reviews:
> "Pretty good!" (4/5)
> "Basic marinara" (3/5)

In this example, we've replaced the call to action ("read more"), which potentially presumes the user is on a browser on a smartphone or laptop, with a more neutral contextualized link, which is better prepared for situations where following links might not be possible (such as on a voice interface) or might dislodge the user from full immersion (such as by unexpectedly forcing them out of the AR experience and into another smartphone app).

Another challenge is the phantom reference "see below." What does "below" mean in an AR context where it could refer to the underlying interface or the physical world around the user? Since it doesn't refer to anything meaningful in an AR context, we can eliminate it by jumping right into the reviews, especially if we're able to pick and choose what content on a product web page to pull into the AR overlay. On a website, the distance between the "see below" call to action and list of reviews might be much longer.

Our final immersion-ready text reads:

> Colavita Marinara Sauce *is perfect for an intimate night in with spaghetti and meatballs and always uses the freshest ingredients.*
>
> *Reviews:*
>   *"Pretty good!" (4/5)*
>   *"Basic marinara" (3/5)*

Making content more channel-agnostic has the core advantage of reducing your maintenance burden and preventing copy from falling out of sync with other copy. But doing so also prepares it for future channels, devices, and technology far over the horizon. We're nowhere near the endgame of innovation in immersive experiences, and when new paradigms inevitably appear, keeping in mind all the possible places our content may end up will pay dividends in the future.

FROM THE ABSTRACT TO THE CONCRETE

Designing, let alone using, immersive content is leagues away from how we handle traditional web copy. Unlike scrolling on a phone, clicking in a browser, or chatting with a voicebot, immersive content is unique. It operates in real, navigable space, rather than the abstraction of devices separate from the world around us.

At its core, immersive content asks us to apply the principles of readable and reachable content in novel ways that stretch the boundaries of what information is to begin with. That can mean writing new content that fits its physical environment like hand in glove, or it can mean rejiggering the same content we've juggled for years to extend its grasp to embrace immersive experiences. But because we have to work with a variety of disparate channels beyond just spatial ones, we need to think about our content multimodally, against the backdrop of a larger omnichannel strategy.

Moreover, we have to balance that overarching understanding with the urgent demands of the living and breathing physical spaces all around us. Many of our old design artifacts don't serve us anymore. They need to be spatial and three-dimensional. They need to reflect how users move through their environment in a variety of contexts. Learning to capture this nuance in the design process is where we're headed next.

4 MAKING FLOW HAPPEN

IF YOU COULD CONVERT your personal website or company's mobile app into a house, complete with rooms and hallways, how would you organize its content and distribute it across the building? Would the foyer provide all the information up front, like the header and hero section of a website? Would the living room be the place with the most important copy, like your about page or portfolio? How would you walk visiting guests through the space? Better yet, how would other members of your household navigate it? Where would they start, where would they go next, and where would they finish?

These are questions architects and interior designers routinely ask themselves about brick-and-mortar edifices—and, as content and interaction designers, we too need to grasp how to tell compelling stories and weave convincing narratives in physical spaces.

One of the most fundamental ideas shared by both architecture and interaction design is flow. *Flow*—the movement of people through an experience—is a core concept in both digital and physical environments. But *architectural* flow through built structures is different from *interaction* flow through digital abstractions. Whereas architects are concerned with how people flow through *spaces* they control, content and interaction designers are concerned with how people flow through both *interfaces and content* they control.

Architects think first and foremost about how to spirit people to where they need to go in a space; accessing information via labeling or signage is often a secondary concern that only surfaces during an interior design process. For us content designers, however, it's our primary concern: how to give users the content they need *while* they move through that space, as effortlessly and as efficiently as possible.

We can use storyboards and flow diagrams to give people what they need, when they need it by first tracing individual journeys through spaces. Then, we can synthesize those individual flow diagrams into collective spatial maps depicting how users circulate through spaces, in the process achieving a more holistic, overarching perspective of our content and its sense of place.

THREE WAYS TO GO WITH THE FLOW

As with web and mobile design, there are many ways to articulate and diagram flows for immersive content. There's no single set-in-stone way to diagram how users flow through immersive experiences, and this book isn't intended to be prescriptive about how you should or shouldn't depict user journeys through content in space. If your storyboards, flow diagrams, and spatial maps are understandable to other stakeholders and teams, you're golden.

But what exactly *are* the three design artifacts I've just mentioned (**FIG 4.1**)? Two of them are probably very familiar to interaction designers, but one—spatial maps—might not be. Let's review them:

- **Storyboards.** Storyboarding is a technique commonly found in interaction design, and it has long had a starring role in VR. We can use storyboards to convert our outlines into "movies" that depict the ideal flows we want to enable, which is very helpful in the immersive realm. Because of

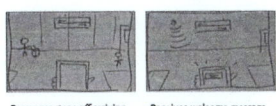

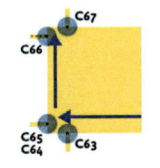

Storyboard   **Flow diagram**   **Spatial map**

FIG 4.1: An example of a completed storyboard, flow diagram, and spatial map.

their pictorial nature, storyboards are best suited to represent user narratives more subjectively—each "scene" in a storyboard can portray whatever we want it to, but, of course, there's no easy way to connect the dots between an individual scene and a single content item.

- **Flow diagrams.** Flow diagrams have long been a fixture of web and mobile app design as a means of bridging the gap between how content items are accessed and what decision points users need to follow to get there. In immersive experiences, flow diagrams organize our content into decision trees capturing both the movements users make (changes in position or orientation) and in-channel or cross-channel shifts (changes in the user's operating context). Because the "card" in flow diagrams generally corresponds to a single content item, they're far more scrupulous in their clarity for stakeholders and implementers alike.
- **Spatial maps.** Spatial maps are schematics of the places we're designing for, indicating where content is located and how users can get to it. They're similar to website mockups, since they're high-fidelity representations of how an immersive environment will actually look with content. To draw spatial maps, we often need access to a blueprint of the space in which we're operating, but a rough sketch of a physical environment can sometimes also do the trick.

There are other design artifacts not unique to immersive design that can be valuable to your process, like user journey mapping. Because journey mapping is a common enough paradigm covered in other literature, we don't talk much about it here. But you can of course adopt user journey mapping techniques and other strategies in your own process to enrich and inform your other design artifacts!

Your project may use one or more of these, depending on your needs; some projects may benefit from using all of them at once. For instance, immersive content with lots of discrete touchpoints on multiple devices and screens would benefit from each and every one of these tactics. But spatial maps might be less useful if you already know where your beacons will be located and how your space will look. Let's dig into how to create each of these artifacts.

STORYTELLING WITH STORYBOARDS

Commonly used in filmmaking to depict end-to-end narratives, running from an initial conflict to the resolution of that tension, *storyboarding* is also an extraordinarily useful tool in immersive content because it's meant to capture the spatial qualities of an environment from the specific perspective of the end user's field of view—rather than from the viewpoint of abstract user journeys or concrete maps of that environment. Because they're so narrowly focused on only what the user sees, storyboards can be especially helpful in understanding how people interact with content in three dimensions rather than in just two, and in motion rather than in place.

As more cinematic, first-person depictions of what users experience, storyboards have their pros and cons. Illustrating in high fidelity what people will do and what they'll interact with might be loyal to how objects in space and the space itself figure in what users see, but it might not be able to surface each individual content item prominently, like flow diagrams typically do. They're also time-consuming to produce and can only depict a single user journey at a time. Nonetheless, they can be a powerfully empathic tool by forcing us to perceive the world through the user's senses rather than our own, whether via sight, sound, or other sensory modalities.

The familiar screen-by-screen storyboard is used by directors and filmmakers to illustrate sets, character actions, and

FIG 4.2: A blank traditional storyboard template, with each empty box representing a different scene in the user journey.

plot elements. Generally drawn in a two-dimensional grid (FIG 4.2), cinematic storyboards are also commonly found in web, mobile, and especially video game design.

In immersive design, cinematic storyboards tie the individual moves a user makes to individual moments in their journey through the space we're designing for. Each box represents an important scene and illustrates a key decision point or state of being for the user, depicting the experience explicitly from their perspective (FIG 4.3). The only hard-and-fast rule in storyboards is to showcase an end-to-end narrative—some tension that needs to be resolved. Everything else is mostly up to you, so long as it falls roughly into the following steps:

Decide what a *scene* is: a key moment in the user's journey where something happens to resolve their conflict or to advance their experience in some way.

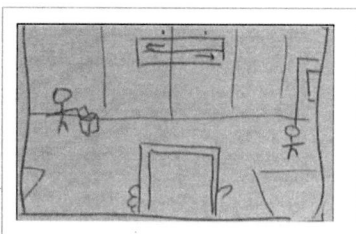

Passenger steps off arriving flight for flight connection	Receives welcome message from airport mobile app
Relocates to new departing gate	Receives predeparture message from airport app on arrival

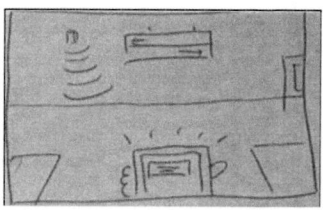

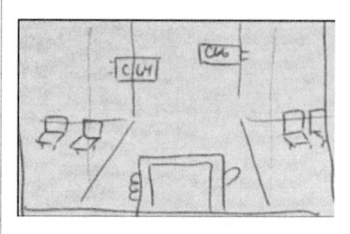

FIG 4.3: A traditional cinematic storyboard depicts the user's flow through an airport as a connecting passenger, receiving locational content at each step of the journey.

Fill in a blank template with a sketch of that scene depicting the most important elements of what the user sees in front of them.

Caption each scene with a description of what occurs in that moment, whether that means content shown, an issue solved, or a new situation.

You might be a terrible sketch artist (like me), but you don't need to be an animator to create a basic storyboard. Nevertheless, if you're worried that your stakeholders might misinterpret what you're trying to communicate, consider adding narrative text that describes the events in each given scene.

While 2D storyboards are excellent for getting a sense of how users will engage with your content and interact with immersive environments, they're not always the best tool for XR design. One of the most intractable challenges for designers looking to implement XR interfaces has been the fact that XR design requires a fundamentally different storyboard approach: after all, there's a third dimension in XR, and headsets introduce the ability to make use of a panoramic or 360-degree perspective.

Panoramic storyboards differ from cinematic storyboards in only one crucial way: the sketches that outline key moments in the user journey take a completely different shape. Instead of boxes, they might be elongated rectangles or elongated circles. But their essence remains the same: a series of scenes, just in three dimensions rather than two. Check out the Resources section in the back of the book to see templates and techniques for panoramic storyboards, which are particularly useful for XR experiences.

Keep in mind that storyboards are imperfect and low-fidelity snapshots of how your immersive experience will look, because they're primarily about telling a story, not outlining something close to an engineering specification in the way flow diagrams and spatial maps can.

SEQUENCING CONTENT WITH FLOW DIAGRAMS

Whereas storyboards present content in the context of a few choice occasions in the user's journey, flow diagrams offer a clear and complete picture of that voyage throughout its progression: beginning, middle, end, and every step in between. Though they feel less concrete and more abstract than storyboards, flow diagrams allow you to organize your content in a sequence that makes sense for the demands of the immersive experience.

Though there are many ways to depict flow diagrams, and this book isn't meant to be super prescriptive, they have two fundamental elements:

- *Cards* represent content (like a message in a push notification or a set of product details) at a point of interest.
- *Arrows* are transitions between these pieces of content.

When articulating user flow diagrams for immersive content, we have to keep track of three types of transitions we depict as arrows between cards: movements, in-channel shifts, and cross-channel shifts.

Movements

Movements are situational changes in space. Even a minuscule shift of weight or a slight turn of the head can be a movement that prompts the appearance of a different content item.

As we discussed in Chapter 2, movements determine what we see at a given moment based on where we are located and where we're looking. Movements can be *positional* (walking from one gallery to another at a museum, say) or *orientational* (shifting a glance from one digital sign to another, for example). We've seen these two adjectives before: remember, headsets that only enable orientational changes exhibit 3DoF, while those that also allow for positional changes demonstrate 6DoF.

Movements in immersive content are the primary means of changing from one piece of content to another; we depict them as arrows between cards. Let's see this in action by using the content from the airport passenger case study to create a flow diagram. In that example, the traveler receives a new push notification at each major point in their journey through the airport. We can slot each notification into individual cards before connecting them with arrows to represent individual movements. In the first card, the user enters the airport terminal and receives a push notification with personalized content welcoming them inside; when the user proceeds to a security checkpoint, they receive another push notification, represented by the second card, with further information (**FIG 4.4**).

Because cards represent not only the content delivered to a user but also the stopping points in their journey where they expect to receive that content, we need to ensure their expectations match reality by mirroring precisely how that journey

Connecting passenger

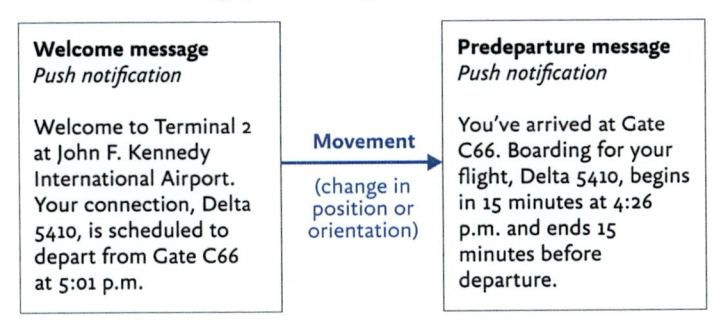

Welcome message *Push notification*		Predeparture message *Push notification*
Welcome to Terminal 2 at John F. Kennedy International Airport. Your connection, Delta 5410, is scheduled to depart from Gate C66 at 5:01 p.m.	**Movement** → *(change in position or orientation)*	You've arrived at Gate C66. Boarding for your flight, Delta 5410, begins in 15 minutes at 4:26 p.m. and ends 15 minutes before departure.

FIG 4.4: A flow diagram showing a connecting passenger moving from an arrival gate to a departure gate, depicted as one movement in locational content from one beacon to another.

---

progresses. In our second flow diagram, we illustrate the universal experience of an arriving passenger with a checked bag (**FIG 4.5**), who needs to conduct two successive movements to access the copy they need. In this case, the arriving traveler disembarks from a plane into an arrival gate and moves to the landside arrivals area before finishing their airport journey at the baggage claim carousel.

It's a good idea to capture as many distinct trajectories as possible and account for them separately, as we've done with our connecting passenger (**FIG 4.4**) and our arriving passenger (**FIG 4.5**), before synthesizing them. In an airport, for instance, most users take a linear path from the terminal to security to the gate. But some users may deviate from that path, especially if they need to do things like drop off a suitcase or print a boarding pass before proceeding through security. First, we can diagram both journeys, both the straight shot and the one with the momentary digression, to make sure we have them both documented (**FIG 4.6**).

Then, we can begin to slot these unique flows together to come up with more comprehensive flow diagrams that are more efficient than a bunch of isolated journeys. For instance, let's take the individual flows we've drawn for each departing

Arriving passenger

Welcome message Push notification		Landside message Push notification		Baggage claim message Push notification
Welcome to Terminal 2 at John F. Kennedy International Airport. You're currently at Gate C68. Your checked bag 02288299812 will be available at Carousel #3.	Movement →	Your checked bag 02288299812 will be available in 6 minutes at Carousel #3.	Movement →	You've arrived at Carousel #3.

FIG 4.5: A flow diagram showing an arriving passenger's single journey, depicted as two movements in locational content between beacons at an airport.

Departing passenger without checked bag

Welcome message Push notification		Airside message Push notification		Predeparture message Push notification
Welcome to Terminal 2 at John F. Kennedy International Airport. Your flight, Delta 5410, is scheduled to depart from Gate C66 at 5:01 p.m.	Movement →	Your flight, Delta 5410, is scheduled to depart from Gate C66 at 5:01 p.m. Boarding begins in 26 minutes at 4:26 p.m. and ends 15 minutes before departure.	Movement →	You've arrived at Gate C66. Boarding for your flight, Delta 5410, begins in 15 minutes at 4:26 p.m. and ends 15 minutes before departure.

Departing passenger with checked bag

Welcome message Push notification		Airside message Push notification		Predeparture message Push notification
Welcome to Terminal 2 at John F. Kennedy International Airport. Your flight, Delta 5410, is scheduled to depart from Gate C66 at 5:01 p.m.		Your flight, Delta 5410, is scheduled to depart from Gate C66 at 5:01 p.m. Boarding begins in 26 minutes at 4:26 p.m. and ends 15 minutes before departure.	Movement →	You've arrived at Gate C66. Boarding for your flight, Delta 5410, begins in 15 minutes at 4:26 p.m. and ends 15 minutes before departure.

Movement ↓ ↑

Check-in message
Push notification

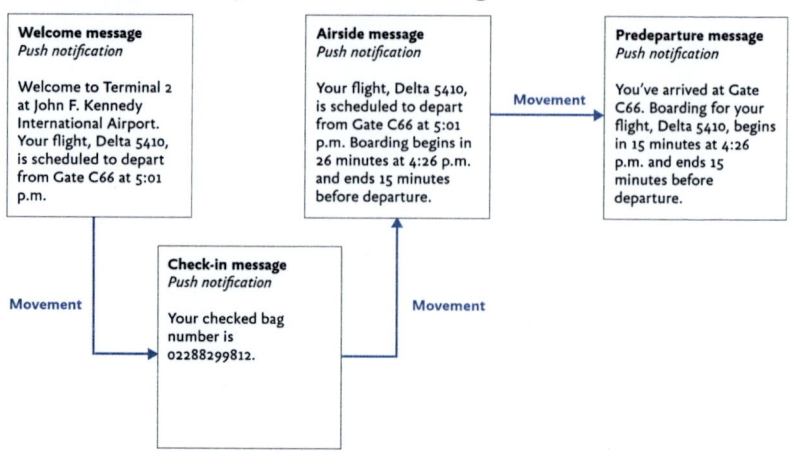

Your checked bag number is 02288299812.

← Movement

FIG 4.6: Two flow diagrams depicting movements between two distinct user scenarios: a departing passenger with a checked bag and a departing passenger without a checked bag.

Departing passenger

Welcome message *Push notification*		Airside message *Push notification*		Predeparture message *Push notification*
Welcome to Terminal 2 at John F. Kennedy International Airport. Your flight, Delta 5410, is scheduled to depart from Gate C66 at 5:01 p.m.	Movement	Your flight, Delta 5410, is scheduled to depart from Gate C66 at 5:01 p.m. Boarding begins in 26 minutes at 4:26 p.m. and ends 15 minutes before departure.	Movement	You've arrived at Gate C66. Boarding for your flight, Delta 5410, begins in 15 minutes at 4:26 p.m. and ends 15 minutes before departure.

Movement

Check-in message
Push notification

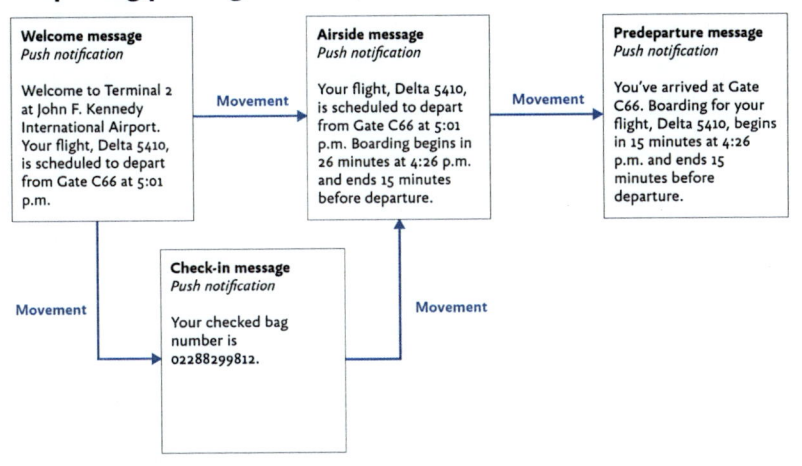

Your checked bag number is 02288299812.

Movement

FIG 4.7: A unified flow diagram combining two distinct user scenarios involving movement: a departing passenger with a checked bag and a departing passenger without a checked bag.

---

passenger's situation and unify them into a flow diagram that illustrates all departing passengers' trajectories in one fell swoop (FIG 4.7).

In this case, whether they need to check a bag or not, departing passengers all start at the same origin and end at the same destination: their flight. This means we'll see some deviation in the middle of the flow diagram but the same shared start and end for all users. But what if the paths users take don't start from the same place or end at the same place? After all, a user could be connecting from an arriving flight and taking an onward flight to a different destination, sidestepping entirely some of the places departing passengers come across content.

Incorporating these separate possible entry points into the user flow is important for the completeness of any cumulative flow diagram. We know, for example, that eventually connecting and departing passengers alike will end up at the same place. This allows us to build a flow diagram embracing both types of

Departing and connecting passengers

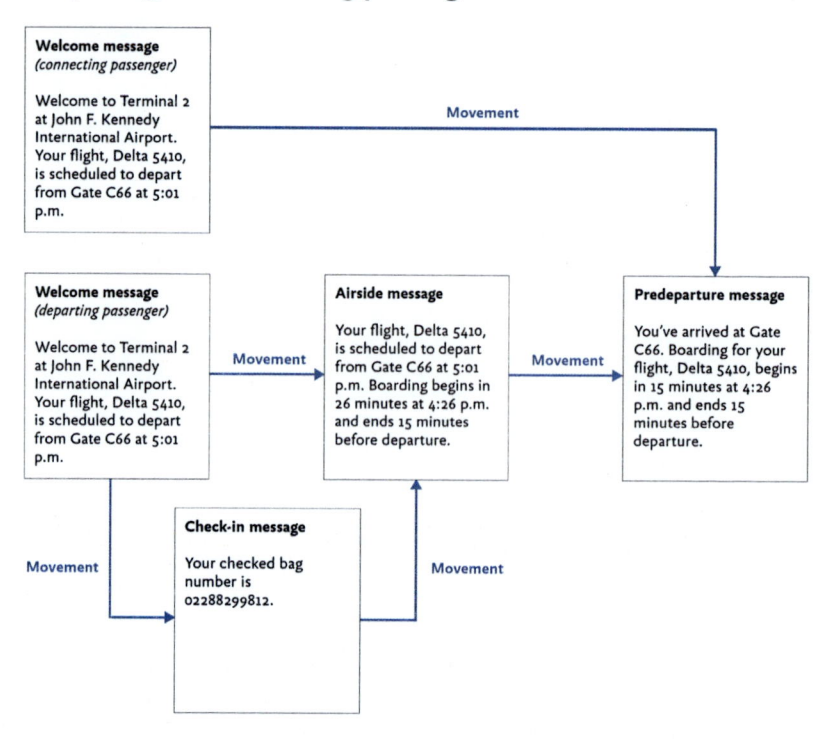

Welcome message *(connecting passenger)*
Welcome to Terminal 2 at John F. Kennedy International Airport. Your flight, Delta 5410, is scheduled to depart from Gate C66 at 5:01 p.m.

→ Movement →

Welcome message *(departing passenger)*
Welcome to Terminal 2 at John F. Kennedy International Airport. Your flight, Delta 5410, is scheduled to depart from Gate C66 at 5:01 p.m.

→ Movement →

Airside message
Your flight, Delta 5410, is scheduled to depart from Gate C66 at 5:01 p.m. Boarding begins in 26 minutes at 4:26 p.m. and ends 15 minutes before departure.

→ Movement →

Predeparture message
You've arrived at Gate C66. Boarding for your flight, Delta 5410, begins in 15 minutes at 4:26 p.m. and ends 15 minutes before departure.

Check-in message
Your checked bag number is 02288299812.

→ Movement →

FIG 4.8: A flow diagram showing both flows for a departing passenger (**Fig 4.7**) and a connecting passenger (**Fig 4.4**), illustrating two separate entry points but one shared endpoint.

---

passengers that finishes at the same endpoint but uses distinct starting points (**FIG 4.8**).

Our airline passenger case study is primarily about push notifications that are embedded, location-driven, and largely delivered in a simple line with minor deviation. But just as the path the user takes could come from multiple entry points or have multiple destinations, what if the user undertakes a wholly unpredictable journey? What if there are so many potential paths that it would be impossible to diagram all their permutations?

Complicating matters even more is the fact that users in the physical world are often much less predictable in their movements than they are on screens, where they're limited to the small array of clicks, taps, scrolls, and swipes we make available to them. But in the built environment, and especially in open-world landscapes facilitating free exploration, diagramming paths with the same level of comprehensiveness as we did for our more straightforward airport can be much more challenging.

As an example, think back to our grocery shopper case study. Shoppers in a grocery store don't beeline between product shelves like they do to their departure gate. They might meander from aisle to aisle based on a jotted-down shopping list or a hunger-induced whim. Because it's impossible to create diagrams depicting every possible aimless, capricious journey, it's far better to limit our scope to representative sample flows. Much AR content found in the wild, such as in art museums, will follow this same approach, whether you're using QR codes or machine vision.

The content in our AR case study was product information—more granular and more substantial than SMS-sized push notifications (**FIG 4.9**). We need to account for a sample of different products on different aisles in the grocery store, with unpredictable movements between them. There are far too many ways a user might traverse these content items to ever document comprehensively, so we just need a few representative samples (**FIG 4.10**). Now, these flow diagrams might seem a bit obvious and oversimplistic—they feel like glorified shopping lists, after all—but the larger the space, the more complicated they can conceivably become.

Because they represent motion through a given space and a change in the user's location, movements are some of the most common interactions we need to diagram in immersive content. They're the immersive analogs of the abstract interactions that govern screen- or speech-based content today: links on a web page, swipes or taps on a mobile app, and messages on a chatbot.

In short, when diagramming movements, you need to document:

Deep River Potato Chips: Rosemary & Olive Oil		Colavita Marinara Sauce		Cinnamon Toast Crunch
Price: $2.99 Rating: 5.0 (1 rating) Evaluations: • "Love the Rosemary!" (5) Description: "Great for entertaining, these chips pack a flavorful punch." Dietary information: None	Movement →	Price: $7.99 Rating: 3.5 (2 ratings) Evaluations: • "Pretty good!" (4) • "Basic Marinara" (3) Description: "Colavita Marinara Sauce is perfect for an intimate night in with spaghetti and meatballs." Dietary information: None	Movement →	Price: $3.99 Rating: 3.5 (2 ratings) Evaluations: • "Cinnamon!!!" (4) • "Not quite as good as I remember, but still nice" (3) Description: "The childhood classic cereal." Dietary information: High Processed Sugar

FIG 4.9: A series of cards in a single journey through a grocery store to pick up three products, with each product's AR overlay displaying associated product content.

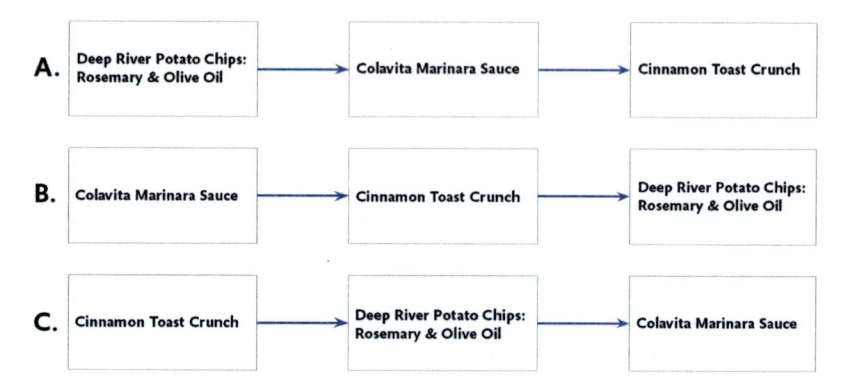

A. Deep River Potato Chips: Rosemary & Olive Oil → Colavita Marinara Sauce → Cinnamon Toast Crunch

B. Colavita Marinara Sauce → Cinnamon Toast Crunch → Deep River Potato Chips: Rosemary & Olive Oil

C. Cinnamon Toast Crunch → Deep River Potato Chips: Rosemary & Olive Oil → Colavita Marinara Sauce

FIG 4.10: Just three representative samples of the many possible flow diagrams that depict unpredictable movements between AR product content items in a grocery store.

1. what a card is, which depends on the irreducible unit of content you need to deliver to the user—the smallest amount of copy they need to continue on;
2. what a movement is, which depends on how your users navigate your space; and
3. what representative sample of flow diagrams will cover enough ground and give you confidence about the possible journeys you enable, especially if they're nonlinear or unpredictable.

Physical movements from one position to another, or one orientation to another, aren't the only way to modify and update what immersive content we see. After all, just because

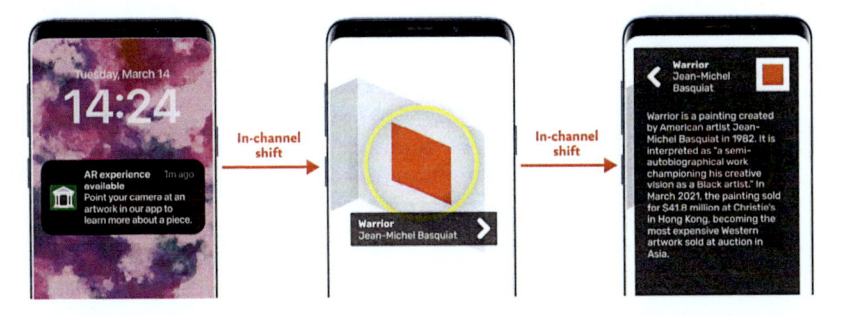

FIG 4.11: Two in-channel shifts occur in this fictional art museum's immersive content App: the first from a location-aware push notification about an AR-enabled gallery to an AR overlay preview of an artwork in the in-app camera view, and the second to an expanded AR overlay with more information about the artwork.

we're constructing content for immersive experiences doesn't mean that we're jettisoning screens altogether. The same scrolls, swipes, taps, and clicks we can do on smartphones already allow users of immersive content to access new content, just as changing their position and orientation do. Those kinds of in-channel shifts are where we're headed next.

In-channel shifts

Unlike movements in immersive environments, *in-channel shifts* surface new content without any change in position or orientation. This could look like hidden content in an XR overlay made visible with a tap, or a "read more" link in a push notification that keeps the user rooted in the same XR headset experience or smartphone app (**FIG 4.11**).

With in-channel shifts, the user doesn't have to change devices or technology entirely. But because in-channel shifts can reshape what the user sees without them changing position or orientation at all, they need to be accounted for differently from movements when they're drawn as arrows in flow diagrams. In this book's flow diagrams, we distinguish between blue arrows for movement and red arrows for in-channel shifts.

A user can plant themselves in the same spot, facing the same wall, and access content through in-channel shifts—in short,

MAKING FLOW HAPPEN **81**

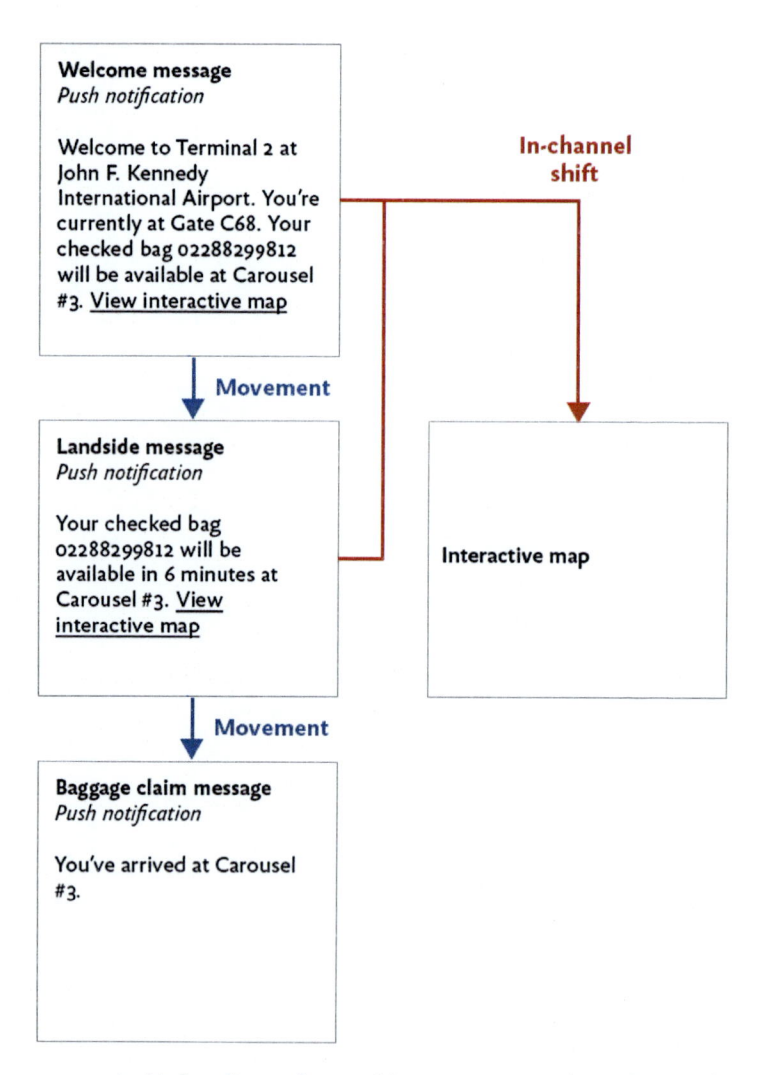

```
┌─────────────────────────────┐
│ Welcome message             │
│ Push notification           │
│                             │        In-channel
│ Welcome to Terminal 2 at    │        shift
│ John F. Kennedy             │
│ International Airport. You're│──┐
│ currently at Gate C68. Your │  │
│ checked bag 02288299812     │  │
│ will be available at Carousel│  │
│ #3. View interactive map    │  │
└─────────────────────────────┘  │
              ↓ Movement         │
┌─────────────────────────────┐  │   ┌──────────────────┐
│ Landside message            │  │   │                  │
│ Push notification           │  │   │                  │
│                             │  │   │                  │
│ Your checked bag            │  │   │ Interactive map  │
│ 02288299812 will be         │──┘   │                  │
│ available in 6 minutes at   │      │                  │
│ Carousel #3. View           │      │                  │
│ interactive map             │      │                  │
└─────────────────────────────┘      └──────────────────┘
              ↓ Movement
┌─────────────────────────────┐
│ Baggage claim message       │
│ Push notification           │
│                             │
│ You've arrived at Carousel  │
│ #3.                         │
│                             │
└─────────────────────────────┘
```

FIG 4.12: In this flow diagram for an arriving passenger at an airport, locational content in the form of a push notification also displays a button that reads "View interactive map," allowing the user to access additional natively linked content within the same mobile application.

this stationary shift in content is what we already do today with the computers on our desks and the smartphones in our hands. We address cross-channel shifts—any appearance of content that obligates the user to switch to a separate device—in the next section.

In our airline passenger case study, when the user taps the "View interactive map" button on their smartphone under the relevant push notification, it opens the airline's mobile app—an in-channel shift within a single application (**FIG 4.12**). This type of transition can be difficult to design because, even though the push notification is coming from the mobile app, the user may not immediately be aware of the connection. In our flow diagrams depicting these in-channel shifts—representing more "traditional" user interactions from a web and mobile perspective—we endeavored to use differently colored arrows to make absolutely clear to ourselves and to stakeholders that these changes in the user's perspective were entirely distinct from physical movements.

Accounting for in-channel shifts is an intriguing issue because it straddles the blurry line between what we consider immersive content and traditional digital content. After all, movements aren't the only ways users typically want to engage with new content, especially in embedded immersive experiences, where they have their surrounding devices at their disposal. Smartphone push notifications, and smartphone camera views too, have the luxury of being able to unfurl into the fully fledged mobile apps governing them that can display more extensive content.

In-channel shifts that point to other content outside the immediate frame of reference allow us to present additional text and media to the user—but it comes at a cognitive cost. Rapid-fire context changes on a device can be mentally taxing for even the most experienced multitasker. And there are some situations where it's far more appropriate to switch channels entirely by expressly *requiring* the user to swap to a different device, like from a smartphone to a touch-screen kiosk, or from a digital sign to a smartphone AR application. Let's talk about these shifts next.

Cross-channel shifts

Simply put, *cross-channel shifts* are interactions that uproot the user from their current channel to access other content. This happens often: when we direct our eyes from our smartphone to an overhead digital sign, we're switching channels. Because immersive content isn't just one channel, but rather a spectrum of possible channels, it's important to illustrate in flow diagrams how users can switch between, say, an AR overlay and a VR wall in an art museum, or a digital sign and a locational push notification on a subway platform (FIG 4.13). Each transition across channels needs to feel cohesive, seamless, and uninterrupted (especially when they're necessarily involuntary), to avoid what Cheryl Platz calls an "interaction cliff" in her book *Design Beyond Devices*.

Cross-channel shifts can be particularly useful for delivering extremely hierarchical content that displays *progressive disclosure*, or greater specificity and detail as the user traverses each tier of content. For example, because digital signs tend to provide broader information to an individual user, more personalized copy catering to users' unique needs is more appropriate for personal devices like smartphones. Just as physical spaces often direct human traffic where it needs to go using architectural cues, in-channel and cross-channel shifts guide user traffic where it's more appropriate by opening doors to other devices and interfaces entirely.

In the airline passenger case study, links in push notifications might take the user to URLs that necessarily open in a web browser—a distinct channel. To depict this in a flow diagram, we can use an additional dimension, or *swimlane*, to illustrate that this type of navigation is wholly distinct from the movements that typically drive access to new immersive content (FIG 4.14). In our flow diagrams, we depict swimlanes as a surrounding box encapsulating all the interactions with content that occur within that channel, whether it's web, voice, or other immersive channels like digital signage.

The boundaries between channels can blur in subtle ways. Oculus, for example, allows developers to build progressive web apps (PWAs) that are, for all intents and purposes, two-di-

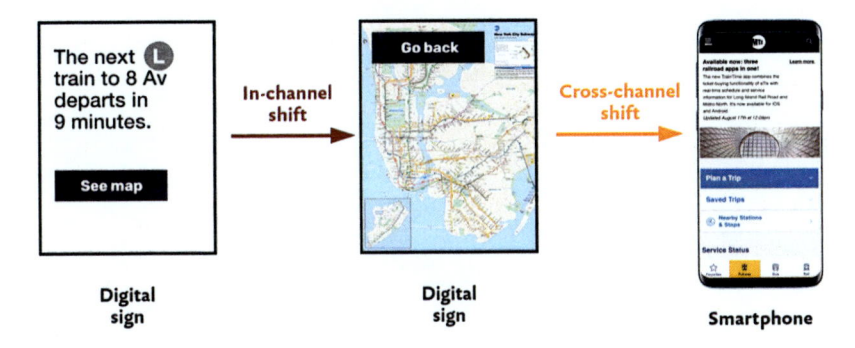

FIG 4.13: To acquire the content they need, users may resort to movements to interact with a different digital sign, follow linked content to find relevant information, or change channels entirely to consult another source, such as a website on a smartphone.

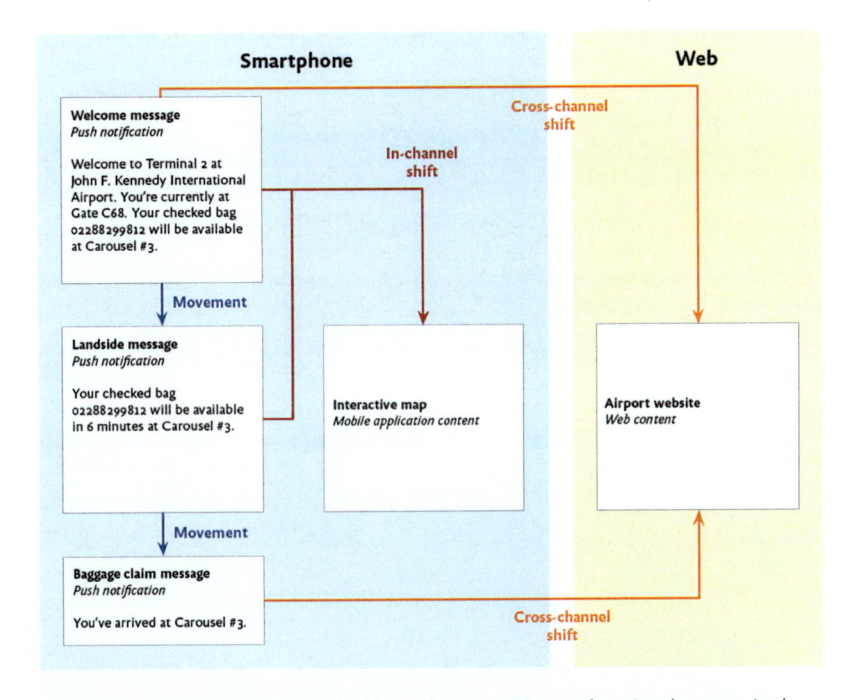

FIG 4.14: In this flow diagram that builds on the one in **Fig 4.11**, locational content in the form of a push notification displays a second button that reads "Visit website," allowing the user to access the airport website in a device browser—an example of a cross-channel shift.

MAKING FLOW HAPPEN   **85**

mensional apps embedded within three-dimensional experiences, like rectangular portals (https://bkaprt.com/icu44/04-01). This makes it possible for designers to interpolate web browsers with working navigation inside VR environments, without making the user feel as though they've changed channels. But is using a web browser within a VR world truly immersive, or is it just patching outdated user interfaces into new contexts?

Similarly, many users are familiar with choreographing the cross-channel chaos of toggling between a website on their smartphone, a digital sign in their line of sight, and a push notification delivered via beacon—all in the span of a few minutes while waiting for a subway train to arrive. But in the near future, thanks to machine vision and XR capabilities, viewing a digital sign through a smartphone AR interface or an immersive VR headset could superimpose a more informative overlay on top of it. But would that still be an example of a cross-channel shift?

That's why, for many immersive content implementations, you might not need to depict cross-channel shifts in your flow diagram. But understanding how your users jump at will between digital channels in search of the content they need in that moment is key to realizing a successful omnichannel content strategy. Using swimlanes to illustrate additional dimensions is one efficient way to display how cross-channel shifts figure into your overarching milieu of content.

As designers and users, we now dwell in a world where the interactions we have with our built environment and with our handheld devices alike tend to overlap in increasingly multifaceted ways. As we toggle seamlessly between a smartphone and a digital sign, a locational push notification and an AR overlay, it gets harder and harder to craft flow diagrams that make sense to users swapping swimlanes at will between immersive content and other forms of information. But this grants us a richly multimodal, omnichannel, and cross-device perspective over all our touchpoints for content, not just one or two of them.

CHARTING SPACE WITH SPATIAL MAPS

Flow diagrams are only capable of illustrating one or a few journeys at once, and they don't tell us much about the nature of the spaces the user is moving through. They slot our users' journeys into a void that doesn't actually exist—a blank expanse that doesn't ever have to contend with walls, distances, or access, unlike the storyboards that often come before them. In immersive design, we have to take things one step further with a third design artifact: spatial maps.

Spatial maps are ways of overlaying flow diagrams into their intended spaces to reveal how the user journeys they depict successfully fill the environment. In architecture, the full set of user journeys we've drawn as flow diagrams is known in aggregate as *circulation*: how people move through an edifice, mediated by "elements that affect our perception of the forms and spaces of the building," as Francis D. K. Ching writes in *Architecture: Form, Space, and Order* (https://bkaprt.com/icu44/04-02).

Compiling spatial maps is a process that can occur before, while, or after your content is written and you have a flow diagram or two in hand. Mapping our spaces allows us to consider holistically all our possible user flows as a collective whole—how users circulate in aggregate through actual physical spaces rather than alone through a blank void. That's super different from looking at each flow diagram in isolation (in the abstract)—rather than in real environments (in concrete circumstances).

Though it's clearly best to have access to a blueprint, floor plan, or other schematic representing the space or spaces you're populating with content, that won't always be possible. In many cases, you may have to sketch your own low-fidelity drawing that only approximates the spatial environment until you can access the real deal during implementation.

Mapping immersive experiences is still new territory, and things are constantly evolving, but there are two basic types of maps I've used in past immersive projects. They can be either two-dimensional, if your immersive content fans across only a single story of a building where users are always walking; or three-dimensional, if it spans multiple stories or multiple altitudes, like the differing FOVs of users sitting down versus standing upright:

- **Point maps.** Point maps focus on individual points where content is discoverable, usually "pulled up" from a single identifiable location. These maps are good for illustrating content in clearly defined spots, like products on shelves or "points of interest" in museums.
- **Range maps.** Range maps identify large ranges of space where content is discoverable—two- or three-dimensional hotspots rather than pinprick points. Range maps are good for content intended to be read from a certain FOV (like digital signage) or based on proximity to a beacon.

Whether your content is embedded or environmental in nature, point and range maps are chiefly about seeking out physical obstacles that might stymie people in our spaces and confirming everything important they need is within their FOV. This is an essential part of the design process: after all, unlike other user experiences involving someone sitting in front of a device screen, it's harder to predict precisely where a given user might be when accessing immersive content. Plus, mapping our content into the environments they'll live in in this way clearly outlines the relationship between a physical space and the content it holds inside.

Point maps

To plot content on a point map, we need to depict each stopping point or juncture at which the user will need to acquire or discover content and later draw pathways between them. But first, we need to start by looking at one of the flow diagrams we just made for our grocery store case study before mapping each of the cards onto points representing each item's location in the store's shelving (**FIG 4.15**). In the supermarket's case, we can't possibly account for every single conceivable product and path, so our point map will necessarily illustrate merely a small subset of the full breadth of available products to choose from. While we'll only draw one point map in this section, you'll

```
[Deep River Potato Chips:    Movement    [Colavita Marinara Sauce]    Movement    [Cinnamon Toast Crunch]
 Rosemary & Olive Oil]       ────────>                                ────────>
```

FIG 4.15: Flow diagram showing one of the possible journeys a user could take across three products in the brick-and-mortar grocery store.

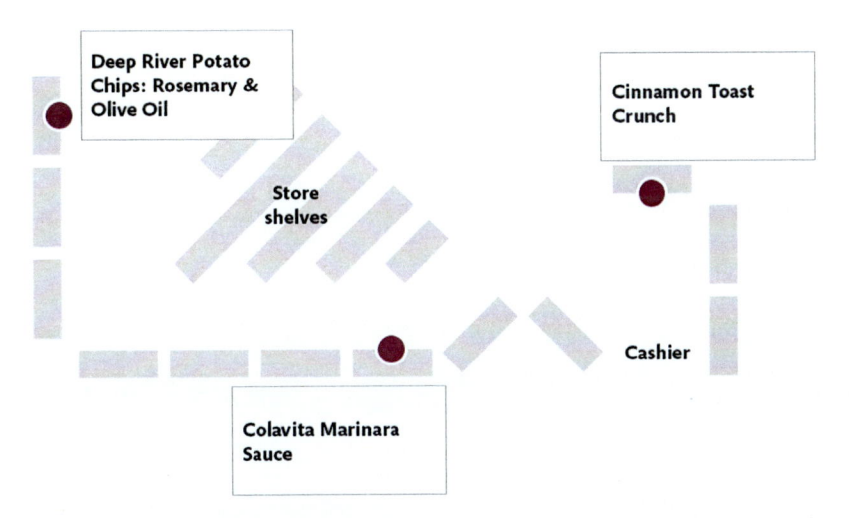

FIG 4.16: A point map consisting of the products shown in the flow diagram in Fig 4.15 and the aisle layout of the grocery store in our grocery shopper case study.

want to account for a diverse array of products and potential paths between them.

Next, we need to layer the flow diagram and its points onto the aisle layout of our grocery store (FIG 4.16). Each point represents a location at which the product is available, such as a dedicated shelf for a particular brand of potato chips or cereal.

Next, let's label each of the points on our point map with the associated content to keep things more understandable. For instance, we can insert a box that contains the same content as shown in the flow diagram with each point. If there's an additional in-channel shift or a cross-channel shift, we can also depict those (FIG 4.17).

MAKING FLOW HAPPEN   **89**

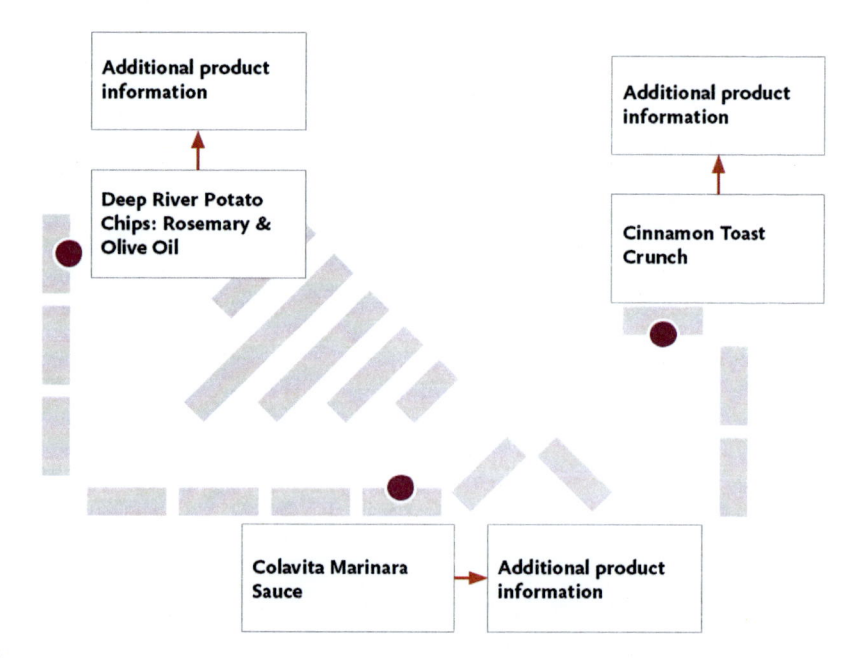

[Diagram: point map with boxes labeled "Additional product information", "Deep River Potato Chips: Rosemary & Olive Oil", "Cinnamon Toast Crunch", "Additional product information", "Colavita Marinara Sauce", "Additional product information", connected by arrows over a store aisle layout.]

FIG 4.17: A point map showing not only the products and their associated cards, but also cards representing the linked content available at each point in space.

The final step is to draw the path a user would take between points by adding in movement arrows (**FIG 4.18**). Yes, just like a game of connect-the-dots! This step is crucial, because while our flow diagrams depicted our users' journeys in abstract space, our spatial maps illustrate the paths taken in the actual physical or virtual environments—such as rounding the corner several times along multiple aisles in the grocery store.

Range maps

While point maps are good for pinpointing specific locations where content is discoverable, range maps are more useful for identifying the sum of all the spots, the swath of space where content is reachable.

Lots of immersive content is necessarily defined in ranges fanning out from a single point, like beacons that broadcast

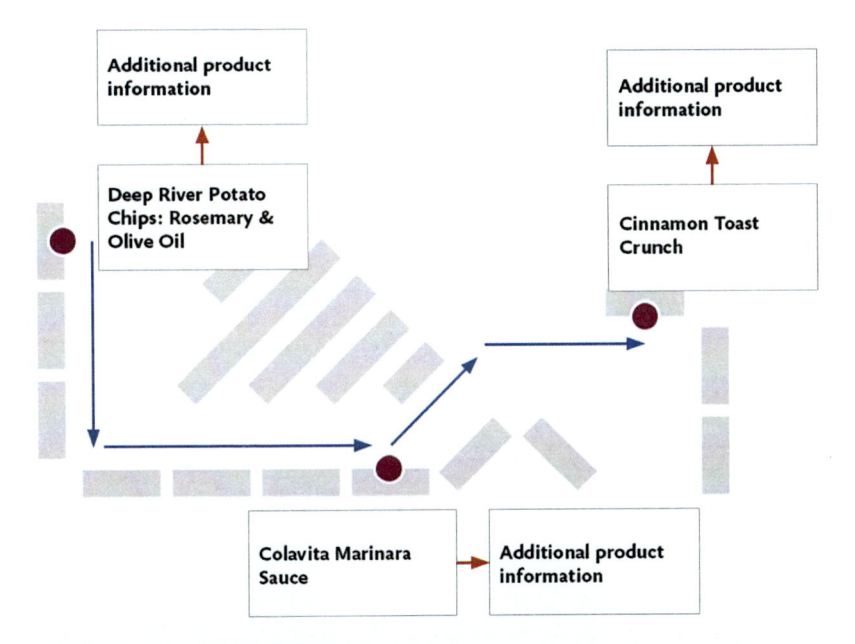

[Diagram: Point map showing "Additional product information" boxes connected to "Deep River Potato Chips: Rosemary & Olive Oil", "Cinnamon Toast Crunch", and "Colavita Marinara Sauce", with arrows indicating the path traversed between points of interest through store aisles.]

FIG 4.18: The final version of our point map, illustrating points of interest, linked content, and the journey traversed to travel between them.

locational content to devices—unlike individual objects scannable through machine vision on AR apps. Locational content, after all, is imprecise; for instance, because GPS can't pinpoint your location perfectly, it instead designates a range within which you're likely to be standing or sitting. By the same token, a digital sign might be better represented as a range within which it's readable at a reasonable distance as opposed to the point where it's pegged into the ground.

Our grocery shopper case study involved points in space because our AR content is only discoverable when viewing it through a smartphone camera equipped with machine vision. On the other hand, for our airline passenger case study, we dealt with locational content that depends on content delivery via Bluetooth low-energy beacons to a user's device. Range maps are a better choice for mapping this content, since there are many possible points to access content within the thirty-meter

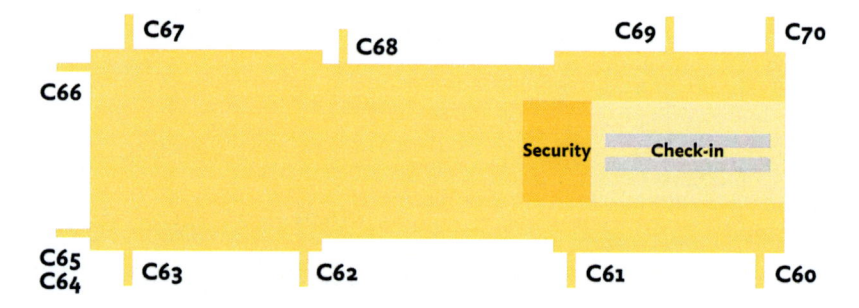

FIG 4.19: A schematic showing a heavily simplified blueprint of John F. Kennedy International Airport's Terminal 2.

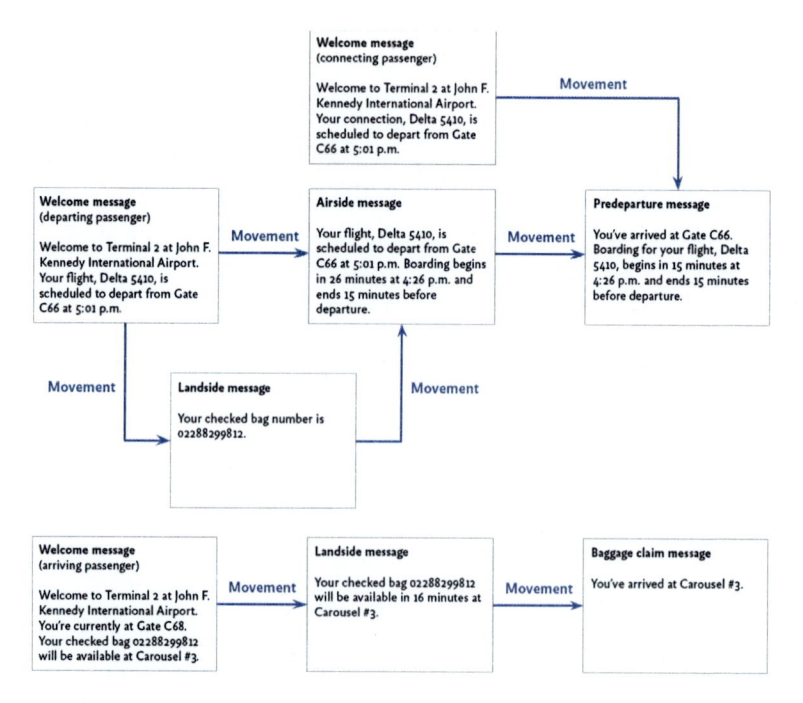

FIG 4.20: A complete flow diagram set that depicts all the possible flows through an airport's locational content.

92   IMMERSIVE CONTENT AND USABILITY

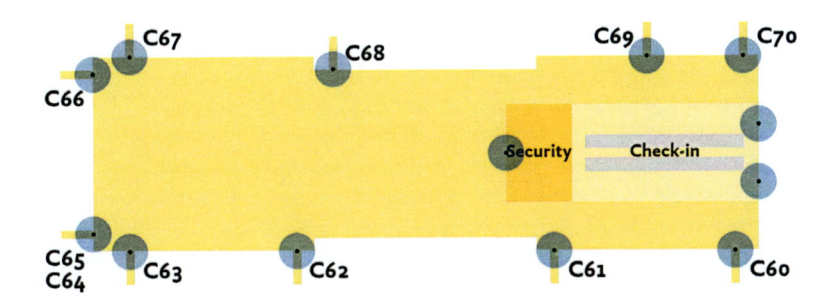

FIG 4.21: A range map for the airport, depicting all the beacons located throughout the facility and their ranges.

range of each beacon. Each range is a circle, past the boundaries of which a beacon's reach becomes spotty—barring any obstacles like thick walls.

If you're designing for an actual space, however, you'll want to use an underlying map of a real facility, like John F. Kennedy International Airport's now-defunct Terminal 2 in our case (**FIG 4.19**). For our airline passenger case study, we kicked things off with a set of flow diagrams charting the user's three most predictable paths through the building: from the airport entrance to a departing gate, from an arriving gate to the airport exit, and from an arriving gate to a departure gate (a flight connection) (**FIG 4.20**).

Because it's cost-prohibitive to blanket the user's entire path with beacons, we needed to focus only on arranging them at each point in the journey where content would be the most useful at just the right moment. In your own spatial maps, strive to reach the minimum viable threshold for your delivery means to avoid going overboard and way beyond what you need. In our fictional airport floor plan, we positioned beacons at the locations representing the airport terminal entrance, each security checkpoint, and each gate (**FIG 4.21**). These represent each place where content can potentially be delivered to the user: at check-in, past the security checkpoint, and at each gate, since each departing gate could feasibly be a location for a predeparture message.

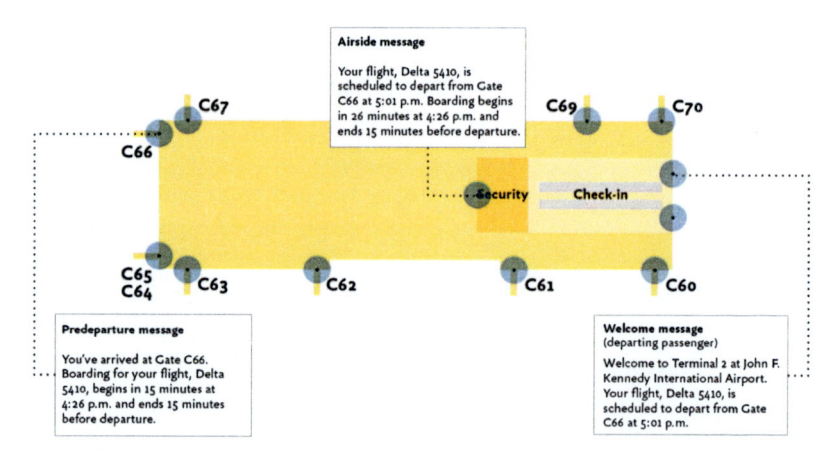

FIG 4.22: A range map for the airport, with two beacons and their associated locational content shown in insets.

As with the point map for the grocery shopper case study, associating each range (or each point at the center of that range) with an inset box displaying the content we're concerned with at a particular location can make your range map more readable to stakeholders and others (**FIG 4.22**), something we did during our design process to streamline reviews. It's a good idea to do this in your own maps too!

Our airport mobile app links the push notifications containing our locational content to other digital properties, such as a page on the airport's existing website. For that reason, we want to depict the linked content available through the push notification alongside the most immediately relevant content we're illustrating in our range map already (**FIG 4.23**). This is just one way to visualize the relationships between your existing digital products and your new immersive experiences, and you might uncover others while making your own maps.

Our final step is to depict the typical paths someone will take between ranges using movement arrows (**FIG 4.24**). Remember that you should do this for all your flow diagrams to arrive at a representative sample of possible paths the user will travel in your physical environment. Each of the journeys we depict

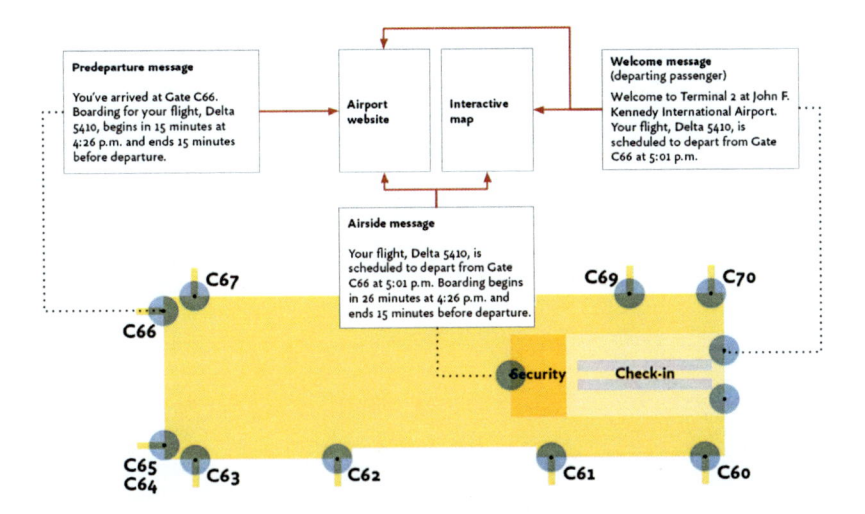

FIG 4.23: The same range map with associated linked content.

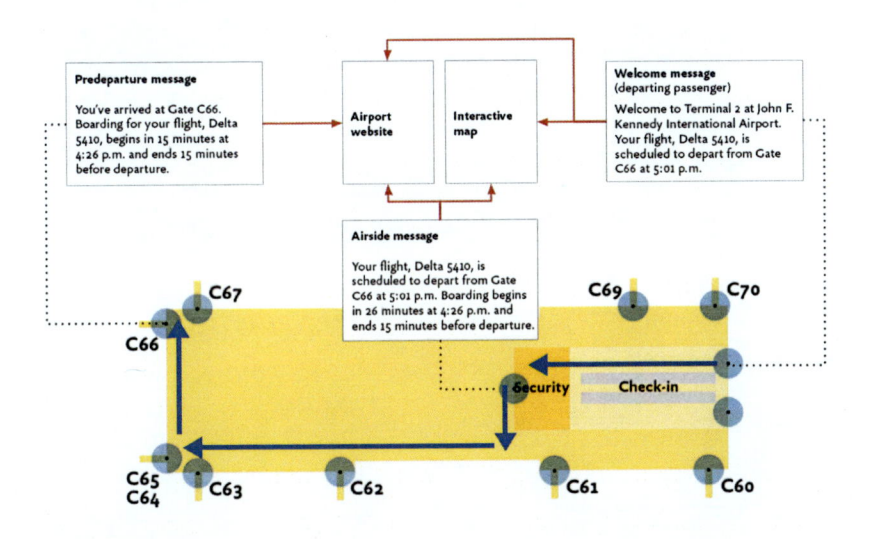

FIG 4.24: The final range map with pathways taken by the user between beacon ranges.

MAKING FLOW HAPPEN 95

through our airport represents a single flow diagram we've put together. But also, just like how having comprehensive flow diagrams for every conceivable journey is overkill, you don't necessarily need to illustrate every point-to-point journey. Just do enough to make sure you're giving what's needed to your stakeholders and implementers alike.

We now have both point and range maps for our content. Not only do they identify precise locations and broader areas where our information is discoverable; they also depict the paths along which our users will encounter that content.

PREPARING FOR LAUNCH

Mapping immersive content is easier said than done, but it's the crucial last step that fully synthesizes the spaces we're designing for and the content we want to deliver to our users.

A point or range map depicting not only where content is legible and discoverable but also every possible journey that users can take across it makes the content you've designed feel real and substantial. It can also be either the final step of your design process before a handoff to developers, or a bookend to another iteration.

But the work to create an immersive content experience doesn't end with implementation. The final hurdle is to take our immersive experience past the finish line by testing it and launching it—in other words, sharing it with real users in real motion—with real consequences.

5 READY FOR LIFTOFF

IN NEW YORK CITY, where I live, our subway system has recently rolled out digital signs—two-sided countdown clocks listing arriving trains, with news tickers along the bottom—across all 472 stations in the network.

While this was a long-overdue step forward for the New York City commuter experience, it didn't come without its issues. The signs were sometimes positioned oddly, seemingly without regard for how and where passengers normally move through the system's spaces. I've found some signs at far ends of subway stations, where platforms tend to be devoid of commuters, leaving the information forever unread. Other signs face walls, or are only legible from near-impossible angles. In the *AM New York Metro* newspaper, city residents commented on the relative scarcity of countdown clocks during their initial rollout—with often only one per station—and on obstacles like ceiling fixtures and other sightline barriers rendering the most crucial content on these digital signs unreadable (https://bkaprt.com/icu44/05-01).

In response, the Metropolitan Transportation Authority (MTA) has tried with some success to relocate many signs, deploying more of them in areas with heavier foot traffic. But the damage was done. Admittedly, it's challenging to roll out digital signage, and tougher still in a subway system as complex, patchwork, and antiquated as New York City's.

Nonetheless, it's a cautionary tale for everyone working on immersive content: without copious testing and careful deployment, you can inadvertently hamstring your user experience. But evaluating our immersive content for its usability doesn't just end with asking whether lines of sight can reach the surfaces of digital signs, or whether smartphone cameras can accurately detect an item. It's also about assessing whether our immersive content performs accessibly for users of all lived experiences—especially disabled users—so the content for our spaces becomes more inclusive and equitable.

TESTING IMMERSIVE CONTENT

Even though this chapter on testing immersive content comes late in the book, consistent evaluation should be an essential facet of your project from the get-go. For example, you can perform content audits not only early in your design process, but also after implementation is complete, to make sure your copy still works on each channel.

At every stage of your project, assess whether your content, flows, and maps truly suit the needs of everyone you're targeting, both with and without them in the room, and whether there are any potential issues that may arise after launch:

- **Testing without users.** When you're just beginning, start with copious user research (ahead of actual usability testing), interviews, and site visits before transitioning to the use of hallway testing, scale models, and simulated spaces that approximate the real experience. All of this testing will give you valuable insights in advance of the legitimate user testing you'll perform later.

- **Testing with users.** *Usability testing* and *accessibility testing* both involve a variety of techniques for evaluating a user experience to gauge its effectiveness. Because immersive content involves motion through space (and in some cases underdeveloped assistive tools), accessibility testing is crucial, especially when it comes to considering disabilities related to vision, mobility, and cognition. Recruit disabled participants from a variety of backgrounds. Keep in mind that immersive content is unique because it operates in real or virtual space, which means testing for a variety of health and safety issues, like accidents and collisions. For imagined virtual environments, test for outcomes like virtual reality sickness and epileptic seizures.

Due to budgetary or resourcing constraints, many organizations elide the critical stages of usability and accessibility testing and gloss over possible health issues. Some steps might not be achievable in all situations, but remember that it's just as essential to advocate for comprehensive evaluations of usability and accessibility in immersive experiences as it is on your existing website.

Testing without users

You may not always have access to the space or people you're building for, and even if you do have those luxuries during the design process, you might be missing crucial basics like connected Wi-Fi, XR controls, or any needed devices and bespoke screens.

That's why the mantra "test early, test often" sometimes means "fake it however you can," just like it does when testing website content. Though they're no replacement for bona fide testing with recruited users, here are a few methods to gather early data when you don't have the advantages of admittance to your site and contact with an actual cross-section of people who will use it:

- **Site visits.** Spend as much time as possible in the environment where your content will live. If you can't work there regularly, try to visit the site often, and bring teammates, stakeholders, or even potential users with you. While our grocery shopper app was still in development, we frequented a Boston supermarket we had a relationship with to test our work in a real environment with typical lighting and sightlines.
- **Scale models.** Scale models are smaller versions of your real or virtual spaces. They help you visualize the flow diagrams and storyboards your users will traverse and allow you to match your spatial maps more easily to the places they depict. Get into an arts-and-crafts mindset when you construct your models. They can be as low-fidelity as cardboard and hot glue or as refined as cinematic special-effects miniatures.
- **Life-size mockups.** With a bit of imagination, life-size mockups can also come close to the real thing. For the grocery shopper case study, we assembled an imaginary grocery store right by our office desks, complete with steel wire shelving loaded with boxes of breakfast cereal, bags of potato chips, and jars of pasta sauce, so we could test right where we worked. And for our airport passenger case study, we installed side-by-side television screens on an office wall to simulate a display in a gate area.
- **Hallway testing.** Chances are you won't have contact with users who accurately reflect your audience until near the end of your project. In the meantime, recruit your colleagues, friends, family, and others to provide feedback on your content. We asked coworkers to participate in tests both during grocery store site visits and in our life-size in-office mockup—and they enjoyed the impromptu work breaks! Keep in mind, though, that informal hallway testing isn't a substitute for formal user testing.

If your project is still in the works, or if site access remains a costly chore, this sort of fakery teaches you how your users might behave before the real deal. But nothing, of course, comes close to a complete round—preferably multiple rounds—of end-to-end usability and accessibility testing.

Testing with users

The goal of usability and accessibility testing is to deeply understand how users will respond to the immersive content you've designed, both under suboptimal conditions and given diverse lived experiences. Your tests should include people who represent the full range of identities, backgrounds, and disabilities, including race and ethnicity, gender identity and sexual orientation, cognitive and physical disability, and more.

Testing with real users under real conditions is important too. *Stress-testing* allows us to see how people will operate in temporarily stressful situations, like severe weather or rush hour—circumstances that test behaviors beyond users' idealized traits. As Eric Meyer and Sara Wachter-Boettcher wrote in *Design for Real Life*, users under pressure, like pedestrians in a hurry or people who have just received urgent news, are perfect candidates for stress-testing (https://bkaprt.com/icu44/05-02).

There are three critical factors to look for in testing: whether your immersive experience is functional, whether it's safe, and whether it's accessible. Scrutinizing just one of these isn't enough—just because it works doesn't mean it works for everyone, nor does it mean it's free of possible hazards like slippery floors or crowd bottlenecks.

Does it work?

Immersive usability testing follows the same broad principles as web and mobile usability testing, with one key distinction: you have to hoof it. With immersive design, unlike with the clicks and taps or scrolls and swipes inherent to the web and mobile worlds, there is simply no alternative to the exertion of physically schlepping around your spaces, in the process trying out the flow diagrams you've crafted and utilizing the spatial maps you've drawn.

But how do we actually do those things? Fortunately, the broad step-by-step sequence of immersive usability testing echoes that of the web and mobile paradigms. After all, all usability tests follow this general series of stages:

1. **Craft optimal test environments.** Ensure you have unrestricted entry to the space where you're testing. If it's a real space, prepare for and minimize potential walk-ins from others, and set clear boundaries around the navigable area users will conceivably crisscross. If it's a virtual space, supply all the equipment users need, such as VR headsets, and provide guidance on how to manage the controls if you're leveraging technology unfamiliar to them.
2. **Recruit test subjects.** Gather a representative cross-section of the population you aim to reach, without neglecting users from historically excluded groups, such as disabled people, Black and Indigenous people, people of color, LGBTQ+ people, economically disadvantaged people, and others. Fairly compensating participants for their time and effort is essential. Without monetary incentives, you might be exploiting those who already face oppression rather than working with them and learning from their insight.
3. **Define scenarios and tasks.** Clearly setting forth tasks allows your tests to be repeatable, and it guarantees the data will be comparable across a variety of subjects and scenarios. Define straightforward tasks by grounding users in a clear set of circumstances, assigning them a mission that needs realizing, and giving them criteria for their evaluation of success. Without direction, your test participants won't know what to do. And if the point of your immersive experience is for users to explore an open-world environment and discover content on their own, give your evaluators their own direction by outlining obvious metrics to track.
4. **Gather data concurrently or retrospectively.** Usability.gov defines two types of techniques to gather data during usability tests: *concurrent* (occurring during the user's interaction with the experience), and *retrospective* (occurring after the interaction is complete) (https://bkaprt.com/icu44/05-03). Depending on whether the user can offer feedback during the interaction without interrupting their immersion in the test environment, use *think-aloud* (where the user shares impressions as they go) or *probing* (where the evaluator asks the user predefined questions) strategies. Consider other means of culling compelling data as well, such as *eye*

tracking, in which a device detects where someone is looking throughout the interaction.
5. **Iterate on your test plan.** Don't forget to adjust your methodology after a usability test is complete. Just as usability testing is most valuable when it occurs early and often, it isn't meaningful without revisions to your process. For instance, multiple times after performing tests on our case studies in locations devoid of other people, we recruited colleagues to simply mill around and act like other users to better approximate a real-life in subsequent rounds. In outdoor environments, we updated our plan to account for inclement weather.

When we conducted usability testing for our grocery shopper case study—both in the life-size mockup we created in the office and at the brick-and-mortar store generous enough to host us—we started by recruiting a wide variety of test participants with a particular eye toward women, people of color, and disabled people. We gave twenty users a smartphone with our app preinstalled, and assigned each of them a shared task and a scenario that had them retrieve lists of items in order of preference:

> *You've downloaded the Fresh Market mobile app and have just set foot in the grocery store. Using the app, scan items from the following categories, read the product description and any product reviews, and choose one for your shopping basket: potato chips, pasta sauce, breakfast cereal.*

To emulate a variety of possible interaction flows, we indicated only the category of the items that users should select from rather than assigning a specific product, especially since we'd built out copy for every piece of merchandise falling into each of those types. This allowed people to make their own decisions about which brand of an item they wanted based on each product's content contained in the AR overlay.

We also wrote tasks that weren't specific to a particular product category but instead looked for shared characteristics across items that would only be discoverable through the AR overlays superimposed onto the detected products people held in their hands:

> *You've downloaded the Fresh Market mobile app and have just set foot in the grocery store. Using the app, scan items from the following categories and choose only those that are rated five stars for your shopping basket: potato chips, pasta sauce, breakfast cereal.*

Writing the scenarios and tasks in this way helped users onboard themselves to the mobile app, and it allowed us to probe both the immersive and mobile user experiences. During the test, we recorded users' reactions by transcribing things they said aloud, tracked whether machine vision was able to identify the item, and noted whether the AR overlay displayed the correct content. After the assessment, we asked users to rate their experience on a scale of one to five along several axes and whether they would use the app again in the future.

Because we conducted this usability test indoors, weather wasn't a factor. But for other projects, such as outdoor digital signage, your tasks and scenarios should consider climatic circumstances that could derail the user experience. Think about how rain, snow, or ice might affect mobility, as well as how sunlight and precipitation might obscure screens with glare or droplets.

Is it safe?

With immersive content, users move in ways that go well beyond the typically tiny gestures they employ on devices. We need to be aware of their physical bodies in space, and be cognizant of how safely they can interact with our content in that space. As you plan your usability tests, scrutinize your immersive experiences for the following:

- **Collisions.** Would any content cause a test subject to have an accident? For instance, test subjects in a supermarket can collide with other shoppers, employees, or shelves. Can you reposition digital signage so users don't run into or block one another, especially out of areas where undivided attention is critical, like the tops of stairwells where accidents are more common? In XR, have you measured whether any critical interface elements in peripheral locations in the user's FOV force them to move too jerkily? Have you measured whether your methods of navigation, like gestures, joysticks, and other input methods, accommodate as little motion as possible to avoid head-on collisions with items and obstacles in the real, nonvirtual world?

- **Traffic obstruction.** In addition to collisions, watch how traffic flows. Consider how test subjects react to locational content based on urgency, such as promotions with countdowns or gamification that requires users to dash frantically around an environment before time runs out. If your digital sign includes a touchscreen component for any connected content, is there sufficient space for users to stop and remain still for a minute or two, or will they cause gridlock?
- **Vestibular sensitivity.** Have you measured whether your VR world or VR interface causes virtual reality motion sickness, or whether any scenes or events induce vertigo or exacerbate symptoms of certain disorders? Isolate any locations where AR overlays may flash in and out, potentially causing epileptic seizures and other health effects. For people with epilepsy, ensure all AR overlays have fade-in and fade-out transitions and that no areas where AR overlays appear on your range map overlap with one another.
- **Ergonomics.** If your AR interface requires the use of a wearable, such as a headset, have you tested whether it's ergonomic and comfortable to wear for long periods? Does it prevent the onset of headaches and accommodate eyewear? Have you examined whether your wearable headset's screen or resolution triggers eye strain? For VR in particular, addressing many health and safety concerns requires balancing the device's own capabilities with the needs of both environment and content.

If people will use your content in a crowded space, be sure to test in one to check for potential collisions and obstacles in traffic flow. For instance, single users walking down unimpeded pathways seldom reflect the real world. Recruit several volunteers to simulate foot traffic in a public space, where pedestrians may walk in front of users or even stumble across their path. Many of the usability studies I've led have included "extras" whose sole responsibility was to mill around a space and move purposefully from one spot to another. Because consuming immersive content is so often concurrent with moving from place to place, we need to analyze how users will juggle all these dimensions of activity at once.

Is it accessible?

Last but not least, your content isn't usable if it isn't accessible. Immersive accessibility remains relatively unexplored, unlike the more mature realms of web and mobile accessibility. Though the past several decades represent a sea change in how we serve disabled people in physical and virtual spaces, thanks to the Americans with Disabilities Act (ADA) in the United States and the Web Content Accessibility Guidelines (WCAG), these are still early days.

Currently, accessibility guidelines remain informal, with loose best practices from individual makers of VR headsets such as Oculus and Microsoft, and emerging advice for XR accessibility from the World Wide Web Consortium (W3C) and invited experts. But because standards for immersive accessibility are still so in flux, there is neither a clear foundation for automated tools nor testing best practices writ large that account for every intersection of immersive accessibility with immersive content.

Your evaluations should nevertheless track accessibility alongside usability. Incorporate accessibility from the very beginning of your project by involving disabled users in the design process, welcoming them as test participants, and compensating them equitably for their time and expertise with monetary incentives rather than taking advantage of them.

The following nonexhaustive list of questions is a starting point (but not the whole story) for identifying accessibility challenges in your content:

- Is your content usable for Deaf and hard-of-hearing people? If there are audio components in your content, especially in XR environments, how are they captioned, and how are the captions enabled?
- Is your content usable for Blind and low-vision people? Is audio captioning available anywhere content is normally visible? Is there other assistive media that conveys the same information, like tactile paving indicating direction for digital signage? Are there refreshable Braille displays or text-to-speech components available for linked content at information kiosks and screen readers for embedded content on devices? Is text that's meant to be read at a distance legible?
- Is your content usable for colorblind people? Does it have sufficient color contrast? Are you using appropriate color palettes, such as light text on a dark background, for variable lighting conditions?
- Is your content usable for people with epilepsy or other vestibular disorders? Does any content come with flashing or strobing that can cause seizures? Do conflicting ranges and overlapping overlays in XR environments cause flickering? Are your real-world and virtual settings both lit consistently?
- Is your content usable for mobility aid users? Can wheelchair, walker, crutches, and cane users navigate your spaces easily? Can they see your digital signage or XR content without significant physical strain? Can users proceed through spaces with content at their own pace, without pressure from external factors diminishing their experience?
- Is your content usable for people with learning disabilities or language challenges? Does your content support dyslexic people by providing sufficient typographic contrast and using typefaces that are both legible and readable? Does your content assist non-native English speakers and low-literacy people by taking advantage of widely used icons and universal symbols alongside text and audio?
- Is your content usable for people with cognitive disabilities? Are your input methods and means of navigation intuitive and easy to understand? Do you avoid presenting users with too many options at once or conflicting information? Do you use understandable terminology, common mental

models already found in the wild, and clear labels for icons and buttons?

In the future, immersive accessibility testing will certainly become just as rich and wide-ranging as it is presently for web and mobile interfaces. But for now, as a general rule, follow the best practices you already might have from experience with web accessibility testing, in addition to the recommendations published by individual device-makers for native smartphone capabilities and for VR headsets—and their input methods.

Just like usability testing, accessibility testing should be a cornerstone of your process, not an afterthought, whether you're writing copy, drawing flow diagrams, or sketching spatial maps. And it should especially be top of mind when first deploying the technology that underpins your content.

LAUNCHING IMMERSIVE CONTENT

Once you've put your content to the test and weighed any usability and accessibility issues that surfaced, it's time to prepare your content for release and place it in front of actual users. Because immersive content involves a sometimes dizzying array of devices and technologies, there's no one approach that covers all the bases. But here a few things all launches share:

- a deployment plan,
- a process for managing and maintaining content,
- quality assurance (QA) testing, and
- tracking user actions and feedback after launch.

Deploying immersive content

By their nature, immersive experiences today entail complex interplays of devices. Whether you need to install Bluetooth low-energy beacons, digital signs, or other hardware, the support of engineering and construction teams familiar with the underlying nuts and bolts will be invaluable. XR ecosystems, too, have their own app marketplaces and procedures for mak-

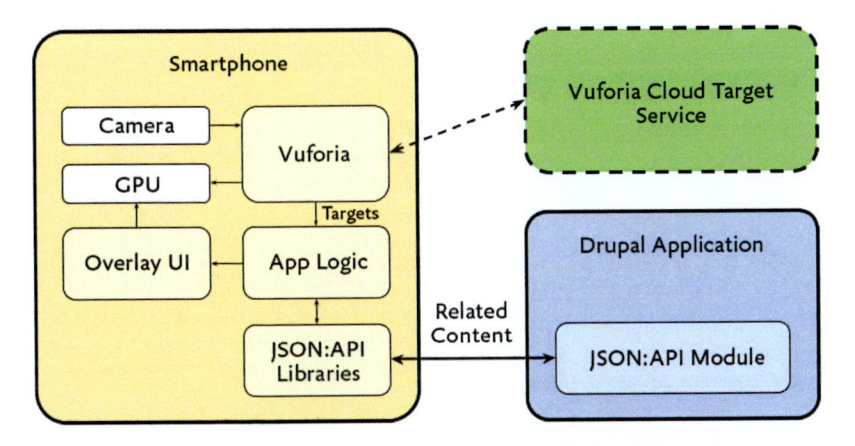

FIG 5.1: The technical architecture diagram for our grocery shopper case study as illustrated by my Acquia Labs colleague Chris Hamper.

ing XR interfaces available to the wider public, which depends largely on the terms and conditions of vendors.

For our grocery shopper case study, as one example, we needed to work with a constellation of technologies for deployment, including a machine vision framework (in our case, Vuforia) and a content management system (the Drupal CMS) to deliver copy to our Android and iOS mobile applications. My Acquia Labs colleague Chris Hamper produced an architectural diagram that served as the basis for our overarching network of technologies (**FIG 5.1**).

In other cases, you'll need to consider how your physical spaces interact with people's devices by using strategically positioned hardware. For our airline passenger case study, though we didn't directly collaborate with an operational airport, when we demoed the implementation, we needed to place beacons in various corners of the rooms we used. Beacon vendors such as Estimote have their own best practices for how and where to place BLE beacons for maximum efficacy.

Digital signage, too, requires careful deployment, especially because it often involves spaces that have existing analog signage or sustain heavy flows of traffic. Today, digital signage implementations range from computers whose content displays on attached televisions to multilayered architectures that rely on tools like Amazon Web Services' Internet of Things (IoT) platform, especially in contexts like train arrival times, where real-time content delivery is necessary.

Many of these decisions can largely be left up to the engineering teams responsible for hardware and software. But it's best not to leave these discussions with technical stakeholders to the last minute, because hardware considerations can have a major impact on both the beginning and the end of your immersive project. You'll seldom make it past the drawing board without a discovery phase in which you frankly discuss what's in the realm of the technically possible with those responsible for building it out.

Managing and maintaining content

One area that content designers often have a bit more influence over, unlike attributes of buildings or technicalities of hardware, is the set of workflows and processes that undergird the immersive content itself. Chances are you already have a CMS that organizes content for your website; if you're reusing content across a variety of channels, confer with your CMS team on how content changes will propagate. If you're creating new content, you may want to store that content in the same CMS, or leverage a separate CMS focused specifically on digital signage and XR.

But that brings us to another challenge: many CMSs are intended for two-dimensional layouts that adhere to a screen-bound paradigm. How does one manage content in three-dimensional space alongside discrete content items in a CMS?

For our college applicant case study (https://bkaprt.com/icu44/05-04, video), which gave prospective students a VR-driven campus tour, my colleague Chris Hamper extended our Drupal CMS implementation to accommodate panoramic 360-degree images and allow administrators to manage points of interest—items and rooms where users could summon text and media associated with those points (FIG 5.2)—as if they were sidebar blocks on a website layout builder or pages in a sitemap tree. He also created a preview interface that showed content

FIG 5.2: In this screenshot from our VR content demo, a content editor uses a version of the Drupal CMS, extended by my colleague Chris Hamper, to edit content for a point of interest, in this case the rehearsal room of the Cornell Gamelan Ensemble at Cornell University, that can be dragged and dropped within a panoramic 3D image.

editors a web-driven version of the VR experience without needing to don an immersive headset themselves (https://bkaprt.com/icu44/05-05, video). Talk to your development team about the possibility of customizing your CMS without having to adopt an entirely new system and risk introducing unmaintainable siloes.

Quality assurance testing

Just before launch, an end-to-end round of quality assurance (QA) testing helps guarantee the best possible experience for your users.

We can put our flow diagrams and spatial maps to further use and gauge our interfaces' faithfulness to spec in QA tests, just like we refer to interaction flow diagrams when testing websites and mobile apps to spotlight any unexpected issues. If your flow diagrams and spatial maps consist of predictable journeys or linear networks, it's worth taking your build for a spin to make sure all hardware and interface elements work as intended. But if you have innumerable permutations of flow diagrams that render end-to-end tests of every conceivable journey impossible, just make your way through a representative subset of your flows.

In my book, *Voice Content and Usability*, I discussed *dialogue traversal testing* (DTT), an approach used in voice interface design to make sure all possible journeys through a voice interface are working as intended. Long story short, DTT, often automated, involves starting from every possible starting point of a chatbot and reaching every possible endpoint, hitting all intervening user choices along the way. With immersive content, though we can't just kick off an automated test without a humanoid robot handy, we can apply the same principles and verify that our content works as intended across all feasible journeys by trialing individual paths in our flow diagrams and spatial maps—spatial traversal testing, if you will.

Your implementation teams might have recommendations for other useful approaches for QA-testing your immersive architecture. For instance, you can perform load testing to determine whether an IoT service and CMS can handle the hundreds of places where a digital sign might appear or propagate content for display within a reasonable length of time. Automated tests that occur in code might also surface potential foibles that will need addressing before launch. In short, QA testing is about ensuring your underlying technology is in tip-top shape and your immersive experience does what you expect.

Logging, reporting, monitoring, and analytics

Finally, incorporate logging, error reporting, and hardware monitoring into your overall architecture so you can refer to a running record of events after launch. Immersive content usually relies on a lattice of technologies to realize a seamless experience for the end user, and so are replete with potential points of failure.

There's another big reason to introduce logging and reporting into your implementation: data collection. To iterate on the final product we release into the world, we'll want to gain insight from usage over time. By tracking metrics—such as how many times an AR overlay is summoned, how often a user is in proximity to a beacon, or how many people pass by a particular checkpoint in a VR world—you can gather valuable knowledge about what your users expect and what they might want in the future.

If you're delivering immersive content alongside your website or mobile app, you might want to unify data and analytics in the same place where stakeholders can consult those of other channels. Keeping it all in a single CMS or analytics dashboard allows you to compare data points such as pageviews, 404 errors, and search queries across all your channels.

ESCAPE VELOCITY

Hooray! You've reached the final frontier of content: true content in space. With the support of iterative usability and accessibility testing (before and after launch), well-performing infrastructure, and ongoing data collection, you'll be able to deliver a robust immersive experience—and build on the progress you've already made.

Coming advancements in immersive experiences may mean you revisit your project earlier than you might think, thanks to accelerating innovation in realms like digital signage, locational technologies, and extended reality. But in the process, we can't abandon the human side of immersive content. How can we ensure our content immerses all of us without putting anyone at a disadvantage?

6 BEYOND CONTENT'S FINAL FRONTIER

OUR ANALOG LIFESTYLES are rapidly embracing experiences that now convincingly merge our screens with the world around us. But our growing fascination with immersive content risks outpacing its ethical considerations. For immersive content to be truly compelling—and safe—for everyone, we can't shove aside what's best for society in favor of what best lines our pockets.

Whether we're talking about the metaverse or about immersive content writ large, designers and developers in our industry still don't look a whole lot like the users they aim to attract. Many people simply can't realize journeys arranged for an "ideal" or "median" user. As Oculus put it in their VR accessibility best practices: "The 'average' user is already being designed for, and very few people actually fit perfectly into the 'average,' if at all" (https://bkaprt.com/icu44/06-01). If we want to create in ways that embrace all lived experiences, we have to acknowledge paths that dead-end, that circle because of indecision, that don't work out the way we expect.

This brings us to our final topic: how to ensure that immersive content reflects our diverse society without aggravating the biases and systems of oppression historically excluded communities already face. Just like hostile architecture in the built environment, the content we conceive can be problematic for disabled people, people of color, queer and trans people, and others.

Content, like hostile architecture around it, always plays a role in systemic oppression. Signage has long discriminated against populations deemed undesirable. Consider anti-Black messaging in the segregation era in the United States and the apartheid era in South Africa, or transphobic signage outside public restrooms. As we design content for a new immersive berth, we must be attuned to how social biases and forms of oppression can transform information into triggers of distress and harm.

Ultimately, immersive content isn't just about how we come across a place and make sense of it; it's also about how we come across our own identities and make sense of them in a larger social context. As practitioners, we can honor the human side of immersive content by focusing on the following:

- Ensure your immersive experiences are private and secure.
- Avoid avatars unless they're truly representative.
- Follow available accessibility standards and best practices.
- Let's walk through each of these in turn.

IMMERSIVE OR INVASIVE?

Let me be frank: I'm torn about some of the technologies I've presented in this book. Immersive content is a revolutionary paradigm for releasing information to everyone, whether they're a choosy customer or a concerned citizen, a frequent flyer or a time-strapped commuter. But without the proper protections in place, whether that means regulatory structures or corporate oversight, immersive content could risk becoming what much web and mobile content is today: invasive.

One of the regrettable truths of beacon technologies and triangulation-driven content is the necessity of location tracking to know where the user is, often continuously, without interruption. Machine vision, too, requires a deluge of data gathered from a wide variety of sources. As the well-documented dangers of doxxing and deepfaking demonstrate, immersive content, like all of today's technology, has the potential to become a threat to our privacy, security, and our basic rights as netizens.

Here's how you can protect your users from harm—and keep in mind these things apply to all products dealing with content, not just the immersive ones:

- **Be transparent about your privacy practices.** Users don't like surprises, especially when it comes to their privacy and security. Be as blatant and as clear as possible about what personal info they're surrendering and how you're going to use it. Give users the option to turn off grants of personal data, or even better, default to disabling it in the first place.
- **Don't lock away features if permissions are denied.** Can a user still access your immersive experience without being surveilled in any way? If you track location to deliver immersive content, is there an alternative that allows more imprecision without alienating the user? Look for ways to engage in graceful degradation of your user experience to protect people who opt out of certain settings.
- **Only use highly sensitive settings if absolutely necessary.** Don't implement location tracking if you don't explicitly need it, and don't gather personal data if the experience doesn't depend on it. Hoarding more data might be better for your organization's bottom line, but it's seldom better for your audience.

While we've seen tentative steps in the right direction thanks to regulatory structures around the world, especially the "right to be forgotten" encoded in the European Union's General Data Protection Regulation (GDPR) (https://bkaprt.com/icu44/06-02), far more work is needed to ensure that immersive content experiences don't lead to unwanted surveillance, abuse, and the erosion of privacy.

THE AVATAR IN THE METAVERSE

Immersive content today rarely asks users to invent a digital version of themselves to access its spaces. But the metaverse has changed that. A *metaverse* is one of many virtual "universes" corporations are racing to build that ostensibly give shape to the abstract online spaces we currently occupy in discrete devices—virtual conference rooms, social networks, and video-game worlds—by supplying XR means of accessing them instead. While the idea has generated substantial hype since its earliest mentions in science fiction, some see metaverses as a meaningless buzzwords that can't come close to replicating real-life experiences (https://bkaprt.com/icu44/06-03). Nonetheless, the notion of a metaverse portends a leap into the unknown, and new challenges for not just content *everywhere*, but content for *everyone*.

At SXSW Interactive 2022, I moderated a panel about accessibility, inclusion, and equity beyond the web with Reginé Gilbert, industry assistant professor at New York University Tandon School of Engineering, and Nikhil Deshpande, chief digital officer of the State of Georgia (https://bkaprt.com/icu44/06-04). Afterward, on our way to the sponsor booths, we chatted with experts working on accessibility and equitable user experiences about the ongoing activism and progress that was realizing tangible benefits for historically excluded people consuming immersive content.

But as we stepped into the exhibit hall, the stunning contrast between our panel and the harsh reality around us couldn't be clearer. Onstage, we'd been met with full-throated support for accessibility and equity; offstage, we were surrounded by well-funded startups proffering blatantly ableist and oppressive products. Our wheelchair-user colleague Molly Bloom trialed a demo from a company that "showed how people could generate avatars with pictures of their faces and biometric data":

> *I pushed up to the demo and took an image of my face and entered my biometric data, including my height and weight. The algorithm went to work, and there I was—an exceptionally slender, incredibly pale, straight-haired person with two legs,*

BEYOND CONTENT'S FINAL FRONTIER 117

in a trendy outfit, no wheelchair in sight. What I saw was an odd reflection of the person that I've worked hard to appreciate.
First, I am, by no means, slender. Rather, I am a combination of muscular and plump. The calculation of body size and stature from weight height that the technology used failed because a substantial portion of my body (leg, buttock, hip, half of my pelvis) have been amputated. Therefore, average measures of body, like body mass index (BMI), are meaningless for me and many of my disabled friends. Second, my skin is by no means as smooth as the soft-focus filter made me appear. Third, though I longed for straight hair as a child, my hair is curly and, more often than not, frizzy. Finally, I have not had two legs for the last fifteen years of my life. The impact of viewing my avatar might have been jarring if I was not used to the mismatch between my experience and how technology producers imagine the humans who will use their products.
I have worked tirelessly to appreciate my plumpness, my blemishes, my frizzy hair, and, especially, my one-legged, wheelchair-using, disabled, badassness. I could not help but smile at the irony of coming from such thought-provoking discussions about equity in technology to this dystopian future in production. [...] The work that I put into finding appeal in a body that does not fit standard beauty norms was erased in a matter of seconds by a technology that had not been designed so a person like me could feel comfortable about who they are.

Lost in our breathless discourse about immersive content and coming metaverses is how to ensure that the biases and forms of oppression we grapple with in society don't take deeper root in our digital landscape. As more companies jostle to assemble their own metaverses, we're having to contend with serious quandaries about how we picture ourselves, how we idealize ourselves, and how we derive our identities, both living and virtual.

The ability for users to generate distinct digital identities has considerable benefits, especially for those who can't come out as their true selves in regular society. For queer and trans people in particular, avatars grant freedom and self-actualization unattainable in the real world. But avatars can also be deeply insidious when their designs mirror or accentuate societal biases.

After all, the control designers have over which identities are idealized over others and which physical features are too cumbersome to include can hamper users' ability to configure and curate metaverse avatars that match who they are. Even worse, imagine a metaverse where there are no disabled avatars, no avatars of color—in short, no avatars that reflect the true nature of the world we live in today. Is a metaverse where we boost select identities over others one we want to accept, let alone inhabit?

HOLD YOUR CONTENT TO HIGHER STANDARDS

As this cautionary tale reveals, inclusive immersive content means supplying information without putting up barriers or propping up biases. While the Americans with Disabilities Act (ADA) enshrines equal access to physical spaces as a human right, there isn't yet comparable legislation for immersive experiences. Fortunately, there's considerable momentum in the World Wide Web Consortium (W3C) for XR accessibility standards (https://bkaprt.com/icu44/06-05) that parallel ongoing work on the Web Content Accessibility Guidelines (WCAG).

Other standards are emerging in the same vein:

- The XR Association has compiled developer guidelines for implementers working in the XR space (https://bkaprt.com/icu44/06-06, PDF).
- Oculus also provides insights for VR designers creating accessible VR experiences (https://bkaprt.com/icu44/06-07).
- XR Safety Initiative (https://bkaprt.com/icu44/06-08) and the CyberXR Coalition have produced standards for accessibility, inclusion, ethics, and safety (https://bkaprt.com/icu44/06-09).
- The Partnership on Employment and Accessible Technology (PEAT) has released recommendations for inclusive XR in the office (https://bkaprt.com/icu44/06-10).

We can also look for inspiration to our existing foundations: our built environment, for example, where we find multilingual signage, Braille, and inclusive language; and web accessibility, where the WCAG set out the widely cited POUR principles for good user interfaces: be *Perceivable, Operable, Understandable,* and *Robust* (https://bkaprt.com/icu44/06-11). Just as POUR applies to visual interfaces on the web, these guidelines can be just as relevant beyond the web in immersive environments like digital information kiosks and XR worlds, where visual and physical interactions can overlap in novel and nuanced ways.

WHERE TO NEXT?

Much of what we can do to make our immersive content inclusive and equitable includes things in our control—like audio captioning in digital signage and XR settings—but that doesn't mean we can necessarily fix every issue that may arise. Because the bedrock technologies underpinning our immersive content are often at the mercy of multinational corporations, it's easy to run up against the limits of our power as individual designers.

It isn't simple, for instance, to modify how XR headsets function for disabled people unless we work at the companies manufacturing them—and even then, our best efforts may get quashed by entrenched stakeholders. Nor is it a piece of cake to renovate public spaces and age-old edifices to embrace accessible constructs like ramps, elevators, and tactile paving (which includes features like truncated domes to alert Blind people to crosswalks or other potential dangers ahead).

That doesn't mean we shouldn't try. Rapid innovation is happening in both the hardware on which we all rely and the software we layer on top. As Chancey Fleet of the New York Public Library stated in *Inclusive Design for a Digital World* by Reginé Gilbert, "XR technology designed with accessibility in mind can lead to innovations for everyone." I'm particularly excited by companies like XRAI Glass, which builds software that transcribes audio into live subtitles for the Nreal AR Glasses (https://bkaprt.com/icu44/06-12).

Meanwhile, tools like SeeingVR (described in Gilbert's book after she saw a demonstration by Yuhang Zhao in 2019) add a "magnifying glass, brightness enhancement, and edge overlays that make a scene more visible" in XR experiences, making them easier for everyone to use, not just disabled users. New joysticks and novel input methods allow for richer navigation without the need for fine motor skills, and there has been a recent surge of interest in haptic content (content that communicates information through touch).

For me, the endgame is true *navigable content*, which I define as "copy and media that can be traversed as if the content *itself* were a navigable space" (https://bkaprt.com/icu44/06-13)—in other words, authentic *content as space*. But we're not there yet. The future of immersive content is still being created and built as we speak.

Since the advent of analog content, we've largely limited ourselves to the humble rectangle—first the borders of the printed page, then the bounded portals of screens. But for the first time, our canvas is reaching assuredly into the realm of tangible territory: the places where we live, work, play, and relax.

In the end, good immersive content isn't about headset gadgetry or grand infrastructure. It's about opening doors to explore new worlds ethically—by enabling everyone to have a hand in creating them, a means of accessing them, and a stake in improving them. Content can only go everywhere when it can truly reach everyone. And that's when immersion becomes immaculate—and feels immaterial.

ACKNOWLEDGMENTS

IT'S BEEN A UNIQUE CHALLENGE to write this book, the spiritual sequel to my first title with A Book Apart, *Voice Content and Usability* (2021), and a hard left turn from my JavaScript book, *Gatsby: The Definitive Guide* (2021). As the world reopened, still deep in the throes of the COVID-19 pandemic, largely without acknowledging our overwhelming collective grief, a new reality (and a severe first bout of COVID-19) dismantled the steady routines I'd built up. To make things harder, instead of writing about just one narrowish topic like voice, I tackled a whole spectrum of immersive technologies that don't always fit together neatly.

Fortunately, I've had an incredible network to buoy me throughout this process, and my latest work wouldn't exist with any of the people who have cheered me on from the beginning and emboldened me to keep at it. This book exists thanks to all of you.

I'm eternally grateful to the former Acquia Labs team, especially Chris Hamper, who was a steadfast engineering partner and architect for all the case studies catalogued in this volume—the grocery shopper, the airline passenger, the high school senior, the new college student. Chris took all our harebrained ideas we first laughed about, then said "hmm" to, then whiteboarded, and made them reality, piquing the interest of so many of our biggest customers. My fond thanks again, also, to Dries Buytaert, Drew Robertson, Leah Magee, Alena "ASH" Heath, and the former Office of the CTO (OCTO) at Acquia for always humoring our oddball ideas and unusual experiments back in the day.

I'm privileged to know some of the most wonderful practitioners and thinkers on the planet, all of whom have deeply influenced my thinking on this subject and on so many others. My biggest thanks to my dear friends Reginé Gilbert and Nikhil Deshpande, with whom I shared a stage at South by Southwest—and I'm especially grateful for all the inspiring conversations we've had over the years about inclusive design, multimodal accessibility, and immersive tech. Also, I wish to express huge thanks to Molly Bloom, who graciously offered to contribute her perspective and insight—without which this book would be much lesser.

My appreciation also goes to the team behind An Event Apart and my editorial colleagues at *A List Apart*, who gave me fertile ground to explore and ample feedback about my initial ideas and distillations. I'll always be grateful to Marci Eversole, Toby Malina, Eric Meyer, and Jeffrey Zeldman for the opportunity to share my work onstage. Thanks also to Ste Grainer, Brandon Gregory, Aaron Gustafson, Bruce Hyslop, and Dougal MacPherson for supporting my article "Immersive Content Strategy" in *A List Apart*, which evolved into this finished product.

Of course, none of this would have happened without the phenomenal crew over at A Book Apart, who've welcomed me back to do it all over again. They've been even more of a joy to work with this time around! My deep and heartfelt thanks to my developmental editor, Greg Nicholl; my line editors, Lisa Maria Marquis and Danielle Small; and my copyeditor, Caren Litherland. And massive gratitude to Brittany Clark, Katel LeDû, Jason Santa Maria, and Leslie Zaikis, who are always such a pleasure to collaborate with.

I wrote this book against a backdrop of considerable challenges when it came to my health. Fortunately, I was extremely lucky to rely on a vast support network of loving friends who lifted my spirits, boosted my motivation, aided my focus, and reminded me why I was doing it all in the first place—whether they did so from New York or Istanbul, Oakland or São Paulo, Denver, or Mendoza. They're far too numerous to list here, but I particularly want to thank my fellow writers Jo Telle and Rohan Zhou-Lee for encouraging and nudging me to keep going. And for letting me lean on them when times were particularly tough and all I wanted to do was put my pen down, all my love goes to Tuğçe Açıkeller, Tuany Cimas de Almeida, Abdul Amunikoro, Diego Aquino, Mark Guzmán, Geoffrey Lee, Mayara Martins, Sheila and Vanessa Martins, Bianca Colombo Mioto, Victor Nils, Michelle Ramiro, and Terrell Woods. I couldn't have done this without y'all. *Teşekkürler. Obrigado.*

Just as I ended my prequel with a personal note, I'll sign off with another here. If you're someone who's faced oppression and historical exclusion in our industry as I have, I hope dearly that leafing through this little tome inspires you to make your own indelible and much-needed mark in the literature. If we don't immerse the world in our lived experiences, immersion might as well be yet another techbro buzzword steeped in privilege and toxicity. The world around us, whether it's real or virtual, needs you to invent it in your image. Ultimately, this book is for you.

RESOURCES

IMMERSIVE EXPERIENCES are nothing new in both academic and industry literature, but immersive content as a discipline remains a relatively niche area of exploration. For this reason, most of the books and articles that are out there emphasize design and implementation topics rather than content design and strategy. Moreover, since immersive technologies differ so much from one another, few resources broaden their scope beyond individual realms like digital signage or extended reality, which translates into a more fragmented landscape for readers.

This book takes a more expansive view of immersive content, above and beyond the territoriality necessitated by isolated technologies. Here are some of the books and articles that shaped my own understanding of immersive technologies. I hope they will be useful to you, now and in the future.

General resources

- My 2021 *A List Apart* article, "Immersive Content Strategy," is a great starting point for content designers and content strategists. In it, I discuss how we should think about immersive content before digging into the specifics of devices and individual genres of immersive technology (https://bkaprt.com/icu44/07-01).
- *Interaction Design for 3D User Interfaces* by Francisco R. Ortega, Fatemeh Abyarjoo, Armando Barreto, Naphtali Rishe, and Malek Adjouadi is an excellent foundational resource for all things three-dimensional, especially when it comes to extended reality. It can be laser-focused on the technical underpinnings of AR and VR, but it's an indispensable guide (https://bkaprt.com/icu44/07-02).
- Another title in the same vein is *3D User Interfaces: Theory and Practice* by Joseph LaViola Jr., Ernst Kruijff, Ryan MacMahan, Doug Bowman, and Ivan Poupyrev (https://bkaprt.com/icu44/07-03).
- *Design Beyond Devices: Creating Multimodal, Cross-Device Experiences* by Cheryl Platz is an excellent introduction to thinking beyond the web or other narrow confines to consider the

unique ability of user experiences to transcend the arbitrary barriers between the devices we carry (https://bkaprt.com/icu44/07-04).

Digital signage

- Though it's clearly beginning to show its age (2010), *Unleashing the Power of Digital Signage: Content Strategies for the Fifth Screen* by Keith Kelsen remains an invaluable tome for those working with digital signage from its early days to the here and now. Ideas we couldn't cover in this book, like screen zones, are more specific to digital signage but still essential to immersive content writ large (https://bkaprt.com/icu44/07-05).
- Paul Flanigan's *The Digital Signage Playbook* offers insight into the workflows and processes involved in typical digital signage implementations with both a number of case studies and ideas applicable to all immersive projects (https://bkaprt.com/icu44/07-06).

Augmented reality

- *Practical Augmented Reality* by Steve Aukstakalnis is a fantastic introduction to the nuts and bolts underpinning augmented reality. It's particularly exhaustive in its treatment of AR technologies, VR headsets, and human factors, especially health and safety considerations (https://bkaprt.com/icu44/07-07).
- *Creating Augmented and Virtual Realities* by Erin Pangilinan, Steve Lukas, and Vasanth Mohan straddles both AR and VR approaches with a focus on both technologies (https://bkaprt.com/icu44/07-08).

Virtual reality

- Jason Jerald's *The VR Book: Human-Centered Design for Virtual Reality* is one of the most comprehensive titles available on virtual reality, with a sweeping overview of design con-

siderations for VR experiences across decades of research and development in VR technologies (https://bkaprt.com/icu44/02-05). *Understanding Virtual Reality: Interface, Application, and Design*, from William R. Sherman and Alan Craig, is another book in the same vein (https://bkaprt.com/icu44/07-09).
- *Learning Virtual Reality* by Tony Parisi is an encyclopedic introduction to the technologies and hardware underlying virtual reality today, with a particular focus on graphics for VR experiences (https://bkaprt.com/icu44/07-10).
- For VR implementations that deal with the built environment and urban infrastructure, *Virtual Reality and the Built Environment* by Jennifer Whyte and Dragana Nikolić is a compelling introduction to the interfaces between virtual reality and the buildings and human landscapes increasingly becoming digitized (https://bkaprt.com/icu44/07-11).
- "UI/UX: Designing for AR & VR" by Nick Lawrence (https://bkaprt.com/icu44/07-12) and "New to VR?" by Raunaq Shah (https://bkaprt.com/icu44/02-06, behind paywall) are useful primers for designers looking to get their hands dirty with design techniques for extended reality.

Design artifacts

From the narrower standpoint of design artifacts like storyboards and prototypes, several articles are deeply instructive:

- "Storyboarding in Virtual Reality" by Vincent McCurley (https://bkaprt.com/icu44/07-13, behind paywall)
- "VR Sketch Sheets" (https://bkaprt.com/icu44/07-14, paywall) and "VR Paper Prototyping" (https://bkaprt.com/icu44/07-15, paywall) by Saara Kamppari-Miller
- "A Storyboard for Virtual Reality" by Andrew Leitch (https://bkaprt.com/icu44/07-16, paywall
- "Simple Low-Fidelity VR Prototyping: Practical How-To Advice" by Michael C. Albers (https://bkaprt.com/icu44/07-17, paywall)

REFERENCES

Shortened URLs are numbered sequentially; the related long URLs are listed below for reference.

Chapter 1

01-01 https://www.cmswire.com/customer-experience/immersive-experiences-be-there-or-be-left-behind/

01-02 https://alistapart.com/article/immersive-content-strategy/

01-03 https://gothamist.com/news/lawmakers-call-more-seating-16-billion-moynihan-train-hall

01-04 https://www.nytimes.com/2021/03/18/science/distracted-walking-phone.html

01-05 https://www.pearson.com/us/higher-education/program/Auks-takalnis-Practical-Augmented-Reality-A-Guide-to-the-Technologies-Applications-and-Human-Factors-for-AR-and-VR/PGM281362.html

01-06 https://developer.oculus.com/resources/design-accessible-vr-ui-ux/

01-07 https://www.mic.com/articles/124899/the-reason-this-racist-soap-dispenser-doesn-t-work-on-black-skin

01-08 https://www.nytimes.com/2020/12/29/technology/facial-recognition-misidentify-jail.html, behind paywall

01-09 https://kotaku.com/pubg-krafton-ai-virtual-woman-metaverse-web3-1849077657

Chapter 2

02-01 https://news.delta.com/parallel-realitytm-unlocks-simpler-personalized-airport-experience-detroit-customers

02-02 https://www.routledge.com/Unleashing-the-Power-of-Digital-Signage-Content-Strategies-for-the-5th/Kelsen/p/book/9780240813028

02-03 https://www.pbs.org/newshour/arts/projection-light-artists-protest

02-04 https://www.techtimes.com/articles/270114/20220105/pr-inwith-corporation-reveals-metaverse-contact-lens-ces-2022.htm

02-05 https://thevrbook.net/

02-06 https://uxdesign.cc/new-to-vr-here-is-what-you-must-know-to-get-started-bc98996ffe46

Chapter 3

03-01 https://developer.oculus.com/resources/design-accessible-vr-ui-ux/
03-02 https://commons.wikimedia.org/wiki/File:Tactile_paving.jpg
03-03 https://shouldiuseacarousel.com/
03-04 https://www.youtube.com/watch?v=I2MuPdt5anI
03-05 https://www.delta.com/us/en/airports/overview
03-06 https://abookapart.com/products/voice-content-and-usability

Chapter 4

04-01 https://developer.oculus.com/documentation/web/pwa-overview/
04-02 https://www.wiley.com/en-us/Architecture%3A+Form%2C+Space%2C+%26+Order%2C+4th+Edition-p-9781118745083

Chapter 5

05-01 https://www.amny.com/transit/subway-countdown-clocks-at-some-stations-are-difficult-to-see-riders-say-1-14115447/
05-02 https://abookapart.com/products/design-for-real-life
05-03 https://www.usability.gov/how-to-and-tools/methods/running-usability-tests.html
05-04 https://www.youtube.com/watch?v=jX4mFkp9vXg
05-05 https://www.youtube.com/watch?v=t_5ZaC8YQ_8

Chapter 6

06-01 https://developer.oculus.com/resources/design-accessible-vr-ui-ux/
06-02 https://gdpr.eu/right-to-be-forgotten
06-03 https://www.gawker.com/tech/i-do-not-want-to-go-to-walmart-in-the-metaverse
06-04 https://schedule.sxsw.com/2022/events/PP115406
06-05 https://www.w3.org/TR/xaur/
06-06 https://xra.org/wp-content/uploads/2020/10/XRA_Developers-Guide_Chapter-1_Web_v6.pdf
06-07 https://developer.oculus.com/resources/design-accessible-vr/
06-08 https://xrsi.org/
06-09 https://cyberxr.org/publication/immersive-technology-standards-for-accessibility-inclusion-ethics-and-safety/

06-10 https://www.peatworks.org/inclusive-xr-toolkit/
06-11 https://www.w3.org/TR/WCAG21/
06-12 https://xrai.glass/ar-glasses
06-13 https://alistapart.com/article/immersive-content-strategy/

Resources

07-01 https://alistapart.com/article/immersive-content-strategy/
07-02 https://www.routledge.com/Interaction-Design-for-3D-User-Interfaces-The-World-of-Modern-Input-Devices/Ortega-Abyarjoo-Barreto-Rishe-Adjouadi/p/book/9781032242842
07-03 https://www.oreilly.com/library/view/3d-user-interfaces/9780134034478/
07-04 https://rosenfeldmedia.com/books/design-beyond-devices/
07-05 https://www.routledge.com/Unleashing-the-Power-of-Digital-Signage-Content-Strategies-for-the-5th/Kelsen/p/book/9780240813028
07-06 https://www.google.com/books/edition/The_Digital_Signage_Playbook/i-GwCgAAQBAJ
07-07 https://www.oreilly.com/library/view/practical-augmented-reality/9780134094328/
07-08 https://www.oreilly.com/library/view/creating-augmented-and/9781492044185/
07-09 https://www.elsevier.com/books/understanding-virtual-reality/sherman/978-0-12-800965-9
07-10 https://www.oreilly.com/library/view/learning-virtual-reality/9781491922828/
07-11 https://www.routledge.com/Virtual-Reality-and-the-Built-Environment/Whyte-Nikolic/p/book/9781138668768
07-12 https://uxplanet.org/ui-ux-designing-for-ar-vr-8c695caccc5e
07-13 https://virtualrealitypop.com/storyboarding-in-virtual-reality-67d3438a2fb1
07-14 https://blog.prototypr.io/vr-sketch-sheets-4843fd690c91
07-15 https://blog.prototypr.io/vr-paper-prototyping-9e1cab6a75f3
07-16 https://medium.com/cinematicvr/a-storyboard-for-virtual-reality-fa000a9b4497
07-17 https://blog.prototypr.io/https-medium-com-michael-c-albers-simple-low-fidelity-vr-prototyping-practical-how-to-advice-a976bd0cdcbf

INDEX

A

accessibility 13-15, 106-108
Alger, Mike 32
Americans with Disabilities Act (ADA) 119
artificial intelligence (AI) 15
artificial locomotion 34
augmented reality (AR) 23-26
augmented virtuality (AV) 23
Aukstakalnis, Steve 13

B

Bluetooth low-energy (BLE) beacons 22
built environment 11

C

case studies 2
    grocery shopper 60-63
case study
    airline passenger 53-59
Ching, Francis D. K. 87
Chu, Alex 32
content delivery 37-41
content in space 19
content zones 32-34

D

Deshpande, Nikhil 117
dialogue traversal testing (DTT) 112
digital signage 19-20
discoverability 49-53

E

embedded and environmental content 8-10
extended reality (XR) 23-28

F

field of view (FOV) 29
Fleet, Chancey 120
flow 67
flow diagrams 73-86

G

General Data Protection Regulation (GDPR) 116
geolocation 20
Gilbert, Reginé 117, 120

H

Hamper, Chris 53, 110
headset vision 28-32
Heath, Alena "ASH" 53
hostile architecture 12

I

immersion 5-8
immersive content 1, 5
immersive content audits 62-63
immersive experiences 5
immersive vs. invasive 115-116
inclusivity 13-15
Internet of Things (IoT) 110

J

Jerald, Jason 28

K

Kelsen, Keith 19

L

labeling 7
launching immersive content 108-111
legibility 41-48
locational content 20-22
locomotion 10-11

M

machine vision 25
metaverse 117-119
Meyer, Eric 101

P

Parisi, Tony 34
phantom references 43
Platz, Cheryl 84
POUR principles (Perceivable, Operable, Understandable, and Robust) 120
progressive disclosure 40, 84
progressive web apps (PWAs) 84
projection art 20
proximity 50

Q

quality assurance (QA) 111

R

reality-virtuality continuum 23
reworking content for immersive use 63-64
Robertson, Drew 53
rotational movement 30

S

safety 12-13, 104-106
signage 7
six degrees of freedom (6DoF) 31
spatial maps 87-96
storyboards 70-73

T

testing 98-108
    without users 99-100
    with users 101-108
three degrees of freedom (3DoF) 30
timing 51
translational movement 31

V

virtual reality motion sickness 13
virtual reality (VR) 5, 24-25
visually induced motion sickness (VIMS) 13
VR locomotion 34-35

W

Wachter-Boettcher, Sara 101
Web Content Accessibility Guidelines (WCAG) 119
World Wide Web Consortium (W3C) 106

X

XR is mixed reality (MR) 23

Z

Zhao, Yuhang 121

ABOUT A BOOK APART

We cover the emerging and essential topics in web design and development with style, clarity, and above all, brevity—because working designer-developers can't afford to waste time.

COLOPHON

The text is set in FF Yoga and its companion, FF Yoga Sans, both by Xavier Dupré. Headlines and cover are set in Titling Gothic by David Berlow.

This book was printed in the United States using FSC certified papers.

ABOUT THE AUTHOR

Preston So (he/they) is a digital architect and strategist, designer and developer advocate, and polyglot educator and speaker. He is the author of *Immersive Content and Usability* (A Book Apart, 2023), *Gatsby: The Definitive Guide* (O'Reilly, 2021), *Voice Content and Usability* (A Book Apart, 2021), and *Decoupled Drupal in Practice* (Apress, 2018).

A globally recognized authority on the intersections of content, design, and code, Preston has been a product, design, engineering, and innovation leader since 2015 at organizations like Oracle, Acquia, Time Inc., and Gatsby. Preston is an editor at *A List Apart*, columnist at *CMSWire*, and contributor to *Smashing Magazine*, and has delivered keynotes around the world in three languages. He is based in New York City, where he can often be found immersing himself in languages that are endangered or underserved.